1989

# You Can Be a Leader:

*A Guide for Developing Leadership Skills*

Candace Goode Vick

Sagamore Publishing
a division of
Management Learning Laboratories

Sagamore Publishing
Champaign, IL, 61820

Sagamore Publishing
a division of
Management Learning Laboratories
Champaign, IL 61820

©1989 by Sagamore Publishing.
Published 1980. Revised Edition 1989.
Cover: Michelle Dressen

Printed in the United States of America

ISBN: 0-915611-19-8
Library of Congress Catalog Number: 89-060961

*Photograph by Charles Howard Cunningham*

Ben and Ethel May Bowers Solomon

This book is dedicated to Ben Solomon and Ethel May Bowers Solomon who believed that ordinary people could be leaders. Ben and Ethel Solomon's destiny was to teach people to be leaders and enable them to train others for leadership. They wanted people to succeed as leaders. They wanted to put in the hands of would-be leaders a simple self-help book on what a leader should be, know, and do. Their goal was to help leaders do a better job, avoid errors, see the results of their work, and find joy in improving the lives of others. Ben often quoted Markham, the poet:

> *"There is a destiny that makes us brothers.*
> *None goes his way alone.*
> *All that we send into the lives of others*
> *Comes back into our own."*

# Contents

# Foreword

To be asked to comment on a well-written book about leadership is humbling. The odds are loaded that one's comments may fail to add anything significant to the author's words. The odds are also loaded that one's image as a leader may suffer by comparison with the qualities of true leadership discussed in the book.

But that is just what being a leader is all about, especially a volunteer leader. You do it because you are convinced that the cause is good and that your joy in being part of the cause will be greater than your fear of making a mistake. You do it because you want to be part of the action, and action is what leadership brings to the cause.

Most of my leadership experiences, both as a volunteer and as a senior staff person relying on volunteers, have been with sport. I have had the joy of seeing a cadre of volunteers lead our Olympians into the opening ceremonies of the Sarajevo and Los Angeles (1984) and the Calgary and Seoul (1988) Olympic Games. Those volunteers had put endless hours of leadership into the awesome aspirations of those marching behind. How many of us can go head to head against the best in our world while tens of thousands of people are watching? How many of us realize that we all can do just that if we clearly define "our" world and know "our" training program?

As a leader, I have also had the joy of seeing the number of quadriplegics from football injuries drop abruptly from some thirty a year to twelve the year after certain rules were changed and then stabilize at five to seven annually. How many of us possess the authority or influence to have such an impact, especially when the opinions of friends and foes alike differ from ours? How many of us realize that we can all make an impact in our world by analyzing, sharing, and taking a position on an issue before acting on it, rather than starting with that position and then merely defending it?

To me, cause, action, and conviction are inseparable elements of good leadership. The author of this book has explicitly covered action and implicitly cause. My contribution lies in adding conviction. This term can best be defined by contrasting it with conformity when we examine leadership styles.

Conformity merely requires that a leader follow certain expectations about style in relation to the circumstances calling for leadership. A conformist can unquestionably be sincere, dedicated, and reliable. But without conviction—the deep-seated belief in a cause, commitment to the ethics and principles of that cause, and the action needed—one may fail to take all the actions warranted under the circumstances. The leader must know the why as much as the what of such actions. Conformity means being willing to go by the rules, but conviction means being sensitive to the why of the rules. Conviction brings empathy, not just sympathy, to leadership.

Empathy means getting into another's shoes to understand the situation and then returning to one's own shoes before determining the course of action. Sympathy means staying in the other's shoes when the choice of action is taken. Drugs that enhance performance, for example, are a source of concern to many elite athletes who feel that their chances of competing successfully are compromised by others who take those drugs. Too many times, however, leaders who are otherwise straight and ethical fail to remind their athletes firmly of the only right position on this issue. Sympathy (by this definition) leaves mixed messages.

Another way of looking at conviction is to think of leadership as coming not from the front (giving direction) or from the rear (giving support), but from the side. Consider the effective drill sergeant who goes up and down the side of his column, directing his attention to the individuals in the group. Those individuals improve only when they perceive what needs to be done and are

x

convinced of its importance. As this book repeatedly emphasizes, anyone (with conviction) who believes a cause to be
worthy can and should become a leader.

Kenneth S. Clark, Ph.D.
United States Olympic Committee

# Acknowledgments

I would like to extend grateful appreciation to both friends and colleagues for their help throughout the process of writing this book. Wile it is impossible to thank everyone individually, without their support and contributions this book would not have been written.

I want to express appreciation to Joe Bannon for encouraging me to undertake this venutre. He has provided helpful guidance during the development of this manuscript and provided the support network necessary to complete it. I also appreciate the assistance of the Sagamore Publishing staff members who were involved with this book.

I would also like to thank the reviewers of the manuscript, Ethel B. Solomon, Dr. Dalton Proctor, and Dr. Violet Malone. Their suggestions and contributions served to strengthen this book. A special thanks to Ethel for the letters and telephone calls that would always come at the time I would need motivation to continue working on the manuscript.

Finally, I want to thank Dennis Vick, my husband. His love, understanding, and advice made the writing this book more enjoyable. I am grateful for his support.

# Introduction

*You Can Be A Leader* was first published in 1981 by Ethel May Bowers Solomon in an effort to preserve the best of Ben Solomon's speeches and writings. For over thirty years Ben and Ethel were the editor and managing editor respectively of *Youth Leader's Digest*, authored over fifty booklets, and lectured to thousands of leaders, paid and volunteer.

This book was written for those who want to learn to become effective leaders in either a paid or volunteer position. It is designed to provide an introduction to the complex subject of leadership. Contrary to popular belief, anyone can become an effective leader. You do not have to have money, special talents, the right job, or any special qualifications to become a leader. You cannot be born a leader, voted a leader, or appointed a leader. You must LEARN to be a leader. Leadership skills can only be developed through hours of training and practice.

Throughout this book, emphasis is placed on leading through influence rather than authority. To be a leader, you must learn how to use your power of influence to encourage people to listen, agree on common goals, follow your advice, and then proceed toward those goals. You must envision what is needed, what is possible, and how to achieve those goals. Without followers, you cannot be a leader, because without action there can be no leadership.

This book is divided into two major parts. Part one introduces basic leadership concepts and skills. Chapter One provides an introduction to leadership, while Chapters Two and Three provide information on what a leader must know and do to be effective.

Chapter Two is designed to teach the reader the difference between influence and authority, gain insight into his leadership style, and begin to understand human behavior as it relates to leadership. The techniques and skills needed to cultivate influence and leadership are outlined in Chapter Three. Chapter Four discusses specific skills a leader must learn to work with four specific groups: children, older adults, the disabled, and the economically disadvantaged. Effective leadership requires that a person be well organized and use time wisely. Time management skills that could be helpful to a leader are outlined in Chapter Five. Practicing good time management skills will help ensure that the reader has a positive leadership experience.

Part Two addresses a special leadership opportunity, volunteering. Valuable leadership skills can be obtained through volunteer experiences. Chapter Six discusses the benefits of volunteering, myths about volunteers, and the basic essentials of a volunteer. The steps to take to become a volunteer are outlined in Chapter Seven. Knowing how to find the right volunteer position to meet one's needs is essential in a fulfilling volunteer experience.

Designed to be a self-help book, *You Can Be A Leader* presents a common sense approach to leadership. While based on leadership theory and up-to-date research in behavioral science, the absence of technical jargon and theory makes this text ideal for use with junior high and high school students, club and class officers, recreation leaders, coaches, volunteers, and youth workers. If supplemented with additional training material, this text could be used as basic training material for leadership development with the groups listed above.

Most importantly, this book is intended to move people to action. Wanting to be a leader is not enough, people must take steps to make the dream a reality. Leadership is an art as well as a science. This book gives the reader the opportunity to develop a personal leadership style by learning, observing, and practicing. You cannot become a leader simply by reading. Knowledge combined with experience can make an effective leader. Checklists and guidelines are included in each chapter to help the reader develop leadership style.

# How to use this book . . .

If you want to use this book to become a leader, I suggest you use the Ben Solomon Method known as the "Solomon Sez" method – SLAPPAM!!! It stands for STUDY, LEARN AND PRACTICE, AVOID MISTAKES. You have to be actively involved with people in order to lead. Everyone must develop his/her own leadership style. You can do this if you follow Ben Solomon's advice and use his three As of leadership:

*A*NALYZE *yourself and the leadership methods of others,*

*A*DOPT *what you find good, and become*

*A*DEPT *at using the techniques you find practical.*

# 1

# Leadership is Influence

*"People cannot be managed.
Inventories can be managed,
but people must be led."*
*-H. Ross Perot, Founder,
Electronic Data Systems*

What is leadership?  When you observe a group of children at play or adults at a meeting it is not difficult to identify  the leader.  However, defining leadership is often a difficult task. Many of us think of powerful, action-oriented people like military leaders, political leaders, and social action leaders. But you don't have to be highly visible to be a leader.  People you come in contact with every day practice good leadership skills. Characteristics of a good leader include patience, understanding, enthusiasm, charisma, good organizational and listening skills, and strength. These characteristics also provide an incomplete picture of a good leader.  They fall short of providing a sound definition of leadership.  There are  hundreds of possible definitions for leadership.   Perhaps one of the most straightforward and easy to understand was given by Ben Solomon, who gave a three part answer.  The first answer was one word, *influence*. While many leadership techniques and skills have to be learned, influence is something everyone is born with. Everyone has the potential to influence someone else. Influence comes from within but you must  learn how to use it. No one can be a leader unless they use this power of influence to move people to action. By leading from behind–suggesting, persuading, and gently guiding others–you exert influence on them.

The second part of the definition is a few simple words. *Leadership is getting people to do what you want them to do.* As a leader you must have the ability to motivate others with their consent, without the use of authority on your part. Although leaders must use authority to motivate others from time to time, a wise leader does not use his or her authority to excess. A leader who is not followed freely is a leader in title only.

The third definition is more detailed than the first two: *A leader is a person who has influence with people, which causes them to listen and agree on common goals, to follow his or her advice, and to take action toward these goals.* There are four important words in this definition: *influence, listen, agree,* and *action.* You cannot be a leader unless people will listen to you, agree on common goals, and take action to meet those goals.

You can be voted into a leadership position or you can be appointed to one, but having the position alone does not make you a leader. Many people assume that if a person is on top the person is automatically a leader, but leadership is not a position or title, it involves skills and abilities. No one can be a leader unless people are willing to follow. You may have authority or power over people because you have wealth, a well known name, or a prestigious job, but you do not have leadership without influence. That is not to say that money, a name, or a certain position cannot increase someone's power of influence, if it is used appropriately. People like Edward Kennedy, Lee Iacocca, Bill Cosby and the president are all leaders, not just because of who they are, but because they can influence people. They can motivate people to action not only with their authority, but because people share their goals and are willing to work toward accomplishing those goals. Once someone can no longer influence people to action, he stops being an effective leader. Authority used incorrectly creates resistance and drives people away, while influence draws people together and creates loyalty. Leaders enable others to act rather than trying to control them. Influence is an important power in the world, greater than law, instruction, and even example. Remember – ideas, thoughts, wishes, research studies, dreams, and meetings don't work – only people of action work. They have the dedication, the drive, and the physical stamina to carry on in spite of delays, disappointments, and defeats.

One of the main ingredients necessary to influence others is credibility. People must believe in you before they will follow you. In leadership, the old saying, "Actions speak louder than words" is certainly true. Your actions – rather than the words you speak – truly show others your values and beliefs. Research has found that credibility of action is the most significant determinant of whether a leader is followed over time. We all know of national, state, and local leaders that have lost their effectiveness when their followers no longer trusted them. They lost their credibility.

To maintain or build credibility with followers, leaders must be honest, competent, and have a sense of direction. Honesty is the cornerstone of credibility. It is difficult for people to have confidence in a leader who has deceived them. Being truthful with your followers is usually the best course of action. To be an effective leader, you must also be competent. Having the knowledge and skills to do your job is important. Your followers must feel that you know what you are doing. It is difficult for people to believe in you if they don't think you have the ability to make sound decisions that affect their lives. Having a sense of direction is also important if you want to develop or maintain credibility among followers. As a leader you must be forward thinking. If you don't have a plan, it will be difficult to move people to action. People look to a leader for direction, and if they don't find it, they will look for another leader. There may be other characteristics that impact your credibility; but honesty, competence, and a sense of direction are the three most important characteristics that will affect your level of credibility with followers. As with influence, you can develop your credibility; however, it is not something you are born with. You must earn credibility through your actions. You can decide which of these characteristics people will use to describe you. I hope they can select all three.

Everyone is born with the potential for leadership in varying degrees. Some people appear to be "natural leaders" because they are always eager to assume leadership roles. Others shy away from leadership roles but are forced into leadership from time to time by an unexpected event. Still another group of people never try to lead. They are always followers, failing to practice or exert their leadership skills. I am sure you can think of people in each of these three categories. However, it is important to realize that no one is born a natural leader. People who appear to be natural leaders have learned leadership skills. They have learned how to use their power of influence. Anyone can be a leader if he/she takes the time to learn and practice good leadership skills.

How does one learn to be a leader? The answer is quite simple. You learn to be a leader just like you learn any other skill or activity. To learn a game such as tennis, you must first learn the fundamentals of the game. Then you must develop your skills through hours of practice and additional training. You must watch for mistakes, correct them, and avoid them the next time. You will need to follow the same steps as seen in Figure 1.1 if you want to learn how to become a leader. First, you must understand what it means to be a leader, and learn the important aspects of leadership and human behavior. Second, you need to know what a leader should do, and the pitfalls to avoid. Finally, you must develop your leadership skills through practice and training. You must learn how to motivate others toward a common goal, how to assess the strengths and weaknesses of your team members, acquire team-building skills and much more on your way to becoming a leader.

**Learn To Become a Leader**

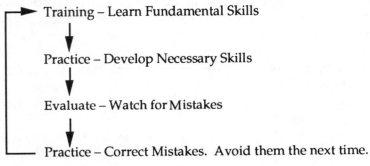

Training – Learn Fundamental Skills

Practice – Develop Necessary Skills

Evaluate – Watch for Mistakes

Practice – Correct Mistakes. Avoid them the next time.

Figure 1.1

Who can be a leader? Anybody! As stated earlier, everyone is born with the potential for leadership. However, many people believe that there are special standards or qualifications for being a leader. They think they cannot be a leader because they are not tall enough, old enough, or smart enough. Nothing is farther from the truth. Leaders come in all shapes and sizes. George Washington was six feet, three and a half inches tall, built like an athlete; Lincoln was six feet, four inches and very thin. Napoleon was five feet, two inches and had a pouch, while Gandhi was very small and thin. What about factors of age, gender, race, religion, or nationality? They are not important. George Washington Carver revolutionized agriculture, and Martin Luther King was a leader in the Civil Rights Movement. Mother Teresa works tirelessly for the world's starving and deprived. You can also be a leader without a high school or college degree. This is not to imply that an education is not important, but don't feel that you cannot be a leader just because you never finished high school or college. The bottom line is that anyone can be a leader if he is willing to develop his leadership skills.

In summary, leadership is having enough influence with people to get them to take action toward some agreed upon goals. Forget the old belief that only a few people are born to be leaders. Leadership opportunities can be found in every part of your life.

The remaining chapters will address various aspects of leadership. Chapters Two and Three will focus on basic knowledge needed for leadership. Information needed to work with special groups such as children, older adults, and the disabled will be covered in Chapter Four. Time management will be discussed in Chapter Five for those who can never find enough time in the day to get things done. Because volunteer organizations provide a wonderful environment for people to practice and develop their leadership skills, the remaining chapters provide information concerning an important aspect of leadership, volunteerism. Chapters Six and Seven will provide information on the benefits of volunteering, the role of the volunteer within an organization and how to become a volunteer.

Good luck as you strive to become a leader. Your journey will take courage, enthusiasm, determination, and study. Rely on the next six chapters to be your guide.

## PORTRAIT OF A LEADER

A leader knows where he is going, why he is going there, and how to get there.

A leader knows no discouragement, presents no alibi.

A leader knows how to lead without being dictatorial; true leaders are humble.

A leader seeks the best for those he serves.

A leader leads for the good of the most concerned, and not for the personal gratification of his own ideas.

A leader develops leaders while leading.

A leader marches with the group, interprets correctly the signs on the pathway that lead to success.

A leader has his head in the clouds but his feet on the ground.

A leader considers leadership an opportunity for service.

# 2

# Leadership:
# What You Should Know

In preparation for a leadership role, there are several important concepts you need to understand. You should have knowledge of the categories of leadership, an understanding of the difference between authority and influence, knowledge of your leadership style, and some insight into human behavior. Of course, this is just an introduction to what you should know to be a leader. Your knowledge of leadership will broaden over time through training, practical experience, and observation of other leaders.

## Categories of Leadership Positions

There are four basic categories of leadership. Each level has its own exclusive duties and responsibilities, its own rights and privileges. In large organizations these categories are clearly defined, but in small organizations there may be some combining of duties. You can begin your leadership experience in any category, but it is often difficult to enter the supervisory or executive categories without previous leadership experience. Many people begin their leadership experience as a person-to-person leader and then move into the other categories.

### The person-to-person leader (direct leader)

At this level, leaders work directly with participants or group members. The 4-H club volunteer leader, Boy Scout Den

Mother, Sunday school teacher, camp counselor, playground leader or teacher are all examples of the direct leadership position because they are in direct contact with program participants. For many organizations, this is perhaps the most important level of leadership because the person-to-person leader is the primary contact with their public. The person-to-person leader is the image builder for the organization. If you would like to be a direct leader, it is important that you realize how important you are not only to the organization but to the people that you work with.

### The supervisory leader

A leader at this level is an individual who oversees other workers and deals with problems they cannot solve. A master volunteer, day camp director, principal, foreman, or a community center director are usually considered supervisors. Without leaders at the supervisory level, many direct leaders would not be able to carry out their jobs effectively. The main job of any supervisor is to get the results that the management of the organization wants. It is also the responsibility of the supervisor to transfer executive policies and directives into the ongoing program. A third and equally important function of a supervisor is to continually try to develop the work of each person to the highest potential.

### The executive leader

An executive leader is responsible for the entire operation of the organization. He or she establishes procedures, sees that policies are carried out and organizational goals are reached. The executive leader is the spark plug that makes the organization run. The director of parks and recreation, executive director of the YMCA, superintendent of schools, and the chief of police are executive leaders.

### The governing board member leader

These leaders are usually lay persons who set policies, define goals, and make it possible for those at the other levels of the organization to carry them out. Leaders are members of boards of directors, boards of education, church councils, and members of commissions.

All categories of leadership are important and require the same basic leadership skills. This book emphasizes the core skills any leader needs to be successful. Those readers in search of additional skills that might be helpful for a particular category are encouraged to seek other leadership references.

You should start practicing your leadership skills in whatever category you feel comfortable and the most qualified. You can practice leadership at work, at home, in your community, and in the organizations in which you are a member. At work, always practice leadership at the level at which you are hired. Don't try to be a leader at levels above you without definite authority from your supervisor.

## Authority Versus Influence

With almost every leadership position comes some degree of authority and responsibility. However, as a leader you should not have to rely on authority to get things done except in rare occasions. A true leader seldom has to give orders, but rather uses influence or persuasion to guide the thoughts, feelings, or behaviors of others. Persuasion involves convincing others that the action you want them to take is appropriate to meet their needs. On the other hand, authority implies that followers will act not because the action is in their best interest but because you have power. The list in Figure 2.1 will help you understand the different methods used by the boss, and those used by the leader. Study the list and let it guide you.

As a leader, there will be times when you must decide whether to use influence or authority. If you decide to use influence, you must convince others that the behavior you desire will lead to the achievement of their goals. If you elect to use authority, then you are depending on your position, title, or people's feelings to determine whether they will follow you. Although leadership by authority is often not successful, there are times when you will have to use your authority to accomplish a goal. In an emergency situation, a lifeguard does not have time to persuade someone to go for help. The lifeguard must use authority to direct the rescue attempt. I am sure you can think of other situations where a leader must use authority rather than persuasion to successfully lead his or her followers. Remember, never use authority in situations where persuasion can be used.

| AUTHORITY | INFLUENCE |
|---|---|
| Authority is the power to act or command, to give orders and to see that they are carried out. | Influence on the other hand is a human quality, an ability to produce an effect in human behavior. |
| Authority (power) can be given to a person by someone else or by an organization and it can be taken away. | Influence is a quality born into every human being and no one else can give it to you or ever take it away. |
| Authority belongs to the position, the rank (and parenthood is a position), and not to the person who happens to occupy the position or hold the rank. | Influence belongs to a person individually for all time. |
| Authority gives orders. | Influence makes suggestions. |
| Authority begets compliance regardless of consent or agreement. | Influence generates willing cooperation, consent and agreement. |
| Authority depends upon force. | Influence depends on reason and logic. |
| Authority demands, pushes. | Influence leads. |
| Authority is one-person rule. | Influence is democracy – "we" in action. |
| Authority generates resistance. | Influence generates cooperation. |
| Authority says "go." | Influence says "come." (follow me). |
| Authority wants its plan fulfilled. | Influence suggests that "our" plans be accomplished. |
| Authority is rule from above. | Influence rules with its followers on their level. |
| Authority offers no choice. | Influence offers choice. |

Figure 2.1

# Leadership Style

You can arrive at a leadership position by various means. You can be elected to a position such as governor, school board member, or mayor. You could also be appointed. Often volunteer leaders are asked to assume a leadership role as a club leader, chairman of a committee, or an advisory board member. Besides election and appointment, leaders can emerge from within the group.

The emergent leader is a person who becomes the temporary leader of a group by virtue of a special talent. This person holds the central position in a group primarily because of group acceptance. Sally Jefferies led a group on a whitewater rafting trip because she was an experienced whitewater paddler. Mike Johnson became the project coordinator for the Volunteer Development Grant because of his knowledge of volunteer systems. Once the activity is over, Mike and Sally will relinquish their leadership roles to someone else in the group. The advantage of being an emergent leader is that you have already earned group acceptance.

Unlike the appointed or elected leader who has to work to earn group acceptance, the emergent leader already has acceptance. The elected/appointed leader is considered a leader by virtue of the title or position. People expect this person to lead because of his position. The major disadvantage of being an elected leader is that he or she must earn acceptance before becoming an effective leader. The members of the YWCA executive board will follow the directions of the newly elected president because of her position in the group. Although to get elected the majority of those voting had to support her, there may be members of the board that do not support her. If she does not keep the respect and acceptance of the majority of the board members during her tenure as president, she will be able to accomplish little. Her followers may become uninterested, work to have her replaced, or follow the directions of an informal leader in the group. This does not mean that all appointed or elected leaders do not have group acceptance. In many instances the person is elected or appointed to the position because he or she is supported by many of the group members. But remember, being appointed or elected to a leadership role does not mean you are automatically a leader.

As a leader you must not only understand the people you are leading as well as the situation, you also must understand yourself. You bring your own personality and values to a situation. In order to gain some insight into your leadership behavior, take a few minutes and complete the T-R Leadership Questionnaire at the end of this chapter. The results of the questionnaire will give you an indication of whether you might be a task oriented leader or a relationship-oriented leader. Don't be concerned if you discover that you are more of a task leader than a relationship leader. The important issue is that you have some understanding of your leadership personality.

There is no single best style of leadership. You as a leader must analyze the situation, the group members, and your abilities before selecting the leadership style that is appropriate for the task at hand. One important criterion that should influence your leadership decision is the maturity of the group members. A mature group can set goals and is motivated to carry out plans to meet these goals. In short, they have the capacity to be self directed; having both job maturity, (the ability to carry out the task) and psychological maturity (self-confidence and self-respect). Mature groups need little if any direct leadership.

If your followers or group members are poorly motivated and unprepared to do the task assigned, then you will have to adopt a task-oriented leadership style. You will have to outline what work has to be done and indicate how and when the work should be completed. Do not spend a great deal of time trying to improve the interpersonal relationships among the group members at this stage. As the group members mature and acquire abilities, you can spend less time directing work activities of the group, and more time on group and individual needs. Your primary goal is to create a group that can operate with minimal supervision. The group will be transformed into highly motivated and skilled group members.

A good example of this group development process can be seen in the almost disbanded church youth group that Mr. Davis agreed to supervise. Although the teenagers wanted a youth group, they did not know how to organize the group or plan the desired activities. First Mr. Davis instructed the teens in how to conduct a meeting and he planned their first teen retreat. As the enthusiasm grew and the teens learned how to work together, Mr. Davis began to slowly give the youth members more responsibility. They organized a Saturday hike in a local state park and planned a trip to the beach. Soon the teens were conducting their monthly meetings and establishing a yearly calendar of events with minimal supervision from Mr. Davis. He is still the official leader of the youth group, but he has gone from being a task oriented and somewhat autocratic leader to an enabler. He helped the teenagers grow. He provided opportunities for them to develop their abilities to solve and satisfy their own needs and desires. Mr. Davis is now in a position to provide the resources and alternatives so that the youth members can select the most appropriate direction for the group.

In summary, an effective leader is one that can match leadership styles to the needs of the group members or followers, the group goals, and themselves. As a leader you will also find yourself assuming many roles within the group. They include communicator, enabler, innovator, dreamer, teacher, motivator, problem solver, and decision maker.

# Human Behavior

### Rule one: people have a reason for participating

As a leader, it is important to understand the people you are leading. There are several general human behaviors that you must be aware of before you can be an effective leader. First, you must realize that people engage in activities or behaviors that will help them meet their needs or achieve their goals. It is up to you as a leader to develop a congruence between your goals and the goals of the group members. The closer the goals are the more likely you will be a successful leader. The group members must see your plan as one that will meet their goals. For example, you are the Youth Director of a YMCA, and you would like to get your teen club involved in a local service project. You know the teenagers come to the center primarily to have fun and socialize. If you can devise a plan that will get the teens involved with the desired service project and allow them to have fun, then you would be in a good position to exercise leadership. Your goal and the goals of the teens will be achieved. Figure 2.2 graphically

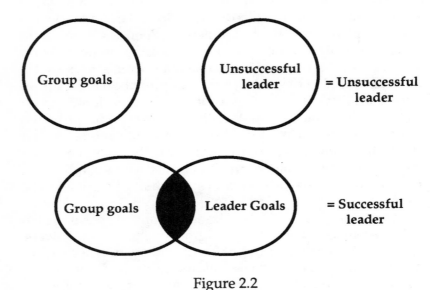

Figure 2.2

represents what occurs when congruence between goals is achieved.

Identifying group and individual goals will not be an easy task. Goals are seldom written down and at times people have difficulty articulating their goals. A good leader will take the time to talk, listen, and observe group members in order to discover their goals. Only then can a leader attempt to satisfy both his goals and the group goals.

## Rule two: people resist change

You must also realize that people are resistant to change. As a leader you will frequently ask people to change their behavior. Be prepared for resistance. The degree to which change is resisted is based in part on how different the new behavior is from the present behavior and the intensity with which the present behavior is held. [Cartwright & Zander, 1968, p. 221]. If the 4-H Club president suggests that club members build a 4-H road sign and landscape the sign area as their community service project, there will probably be little resistance because the 4-H members have done that type of work before. If the leader asks all the club members to compete in the county presentation program, there would be a great deal of resistance from the group. Standing up in front of three judges and delivering a 12 minute presentation is a new and different experience for most children ages 9 to 12. Various members of the group may resist in varying degrees. The members who participated last year in the county presentation day may be more willing to participate than the 4-H members who have never participated in the presentation program. The ones who have never participated may hold their position and refuse to participate.

## Rule three: people are different

Participants come into a group with their own set of beliefs, values, attitudes, feelings, and life experiences. Group members may have different religious beliefs, levels of education, financial status, or levels of wellness. You must be aware of these differences if you are going to successfully lead the group.

As a leader you must periodically assess group goals and needs, your goals, and the situation. As you move to the next chapter, it is important you realize that "...no one knows for certain how to prepare leaders... There are no magical formulas, no tried and true recipes, no perfect models, and no guarantees... Leadership is an art and a science." [Heller, 1974, p. 7]. In the following chapter you will discover how to be a leader, how to develop your influence, and the basic techniques that can make your leadership roles pleasant and successful.

## Leadership Questionnaire

The following items describe aspects of leadership behavior. Respond to each item according to the way you would most likely act if you were the leader of a group. Circle whether you would most likely behave in the described way:  A = always, F = frequently, O = occasionally, S = seldom, or N = never.

1. I would most likely act as the spokesperson of the group.    A  F  O  S  N
2. I would encourage overtime work.    A  F  O  S  N
3. I would allow group members complete freedom in their work.    A  F  O  S  N
4. I would encourage the use of uniform procedures.    A  F  O  S  N
5. I would permit the group members to use their own judgment in solving problems.    A  F  O  S  N
6. I would stress being ahead of competing groups.    A  F  O  S  N
7. I would speak as a representative of the group.    A  F  O  S  N
8. I would needle members for greater effort.    A  F  O  S  N
9. I would try out my ideas in the group.    A  F  O  S  N
10. I would let the group members do their work the way they think best.    A  F  O  S  N
11. I would be working hard for a promotion.    A  F  O  S  N
12. I would tolerate postponement and uncertainty.    A  F  O  S  N
13. I would speak for the group if there were visitors present.    A  F  O  S  N
14. I would keep the work moving at a rapid pace.    A  F  O  S  N
15. I would turn the members loose on a job and let them go to it.    A  F  O  S  N
16. I would settle conflicts when they occur in the group.    A  F  O  S  N
17. I would get swamped by details.    A  F  O  S  N
18. I would represent the group at outside meetings.    A  F  O  S  N
19. I would be reluctant to allow the members any freedom of action.    A  F  O  S  N

20. I would decide what should be
    done and how it should be done.        A    F    O    S    N
21. I would push for increased
    productivity.                          A    F    O    S    N
22. I would let some members have
    authority that I could keep.           A    F    O    S    N
23. Things would usually turn out as
    I had predicted.                       A    F    O    S    N
24. I would allow the group a high
    degree of initiative.                  A    F    O    S    N
25. I would assign group members
    to particular tasks.                   A    F    O    S    N
26. I would be willing to make changes.    A    F    O    S    N
27. I would ask the members to
    work harder.                           A    F    O    S    N
28. I would trust the group members to
    exercise good judgment.                A    F    O    S    N
29. I would schedule the work to
    be done.                               A    F    O    S    N
30. I would persuade others that my
    ideas are to their advantage.          A    F    O    S    N
31. I would permit the group to set
    its own pace.                          A    F    O    S    N
32. I would urge the group to beat its
    previous levels of productivity.       A    F    O    S    N
33. I would act without consulting
    the group.                             A    F    O    S    N
34. I would ask that group members fol-
    low standard rules and regulations.    A    F    O    S    N

Score as follows:

1. Circle the item number for items 8, 12, 17, 18, 19, 30, 33, and 34.
2. Write the number 1 in front of a circled item number if you responded S or N to that item.
3. Also write a number 1 infront of an item number not circled if you responded A or F.
4. Circle the number of 1s that you have written in front of the following items: 3, 5, 8, 10, 15, 18, 19, 22, 24, 26, 28, 30, 31, 33, 34.
5. Count the circled number of 1s-This is your score for concern for relationships.
6. Count the uncircled number 1s. This is your score for concern for task.

(Taken from Russell, R.V. 1986. Instructors Manual to Accompany *Leadership in Recreation*. Adapted from Pfeiffer, Wiliams and Jones, 1974. *A Handbook of Structured Experiences for Human Relations Training*, Volume 1. La Jolla, California University Associates.)

# 3

# Leadership: What You Should Do

The advice in this chapter is organized to help you learn how to become a leader. In the following pages, you will be introduced to the skills you need to develop as a leader.

## Cultivating Influence

There are general methods of leadership and specific techniques that will help you cultivate your influence. Without influence a leader must resort to using authority to get things done. You cannot be successful in attaining the goals of a group, organization, or society without cooperation from others. As a leader you must learn to organize, direct, and coordinate the efforts of others, set goals, maintain the group, handle conflict, and much more. Don't confuse leadership with being an instructor. Leadership goes beyond teaching a skill. This is not to say that instructors are not leaders or that leaders do not teach. As a leader you have a responsibility to teach your followers skills and values, but your leadership goes beyond just teaching. As an instructor you are interested in the activity or task, but you also have to be person-centered. Many teachers or instructors are good leaders and incorporate leadership techniques into their teaching. They would consider themselves leaders as well as teachers. As you practice your leadership skills, periodically review the chart below. If you find that you are operating more

## WHICH ARE YOU?
## AN INSTRUCTOR OR A LEADER?

| INSTRUCTOR | LEADER |
|---|---|
| 1. An instructor's job is to teach a skill, a technique, an activity, a game or a subject. | 1. A leader's job is to influence the growth of the followers to better citizenship. |
| 2. His or her main aim is to improve the skill of the individual. | 2. A leader's main aim is to improve character and life. |
| 3. An instructor is primarily activity-centered. | 3. A leader is person-centered as well as activity-oriented. |
| 4. Instructors are mainly concerned with how well a person can perform now, in the activity or game. | 4. A leader is more concerned by how well people will perform in adulthood, what ideals, what values, what goals they will reach for. |
| 5. Instructors watch what is happening to the ball and its effect on the scoreboard. | 5. A leader is concerned with what is happening to the followers. |
| 6. Instructors want results now. | 6. A leader aims for results in the future. |
| 7. An instructor stresses and uses position, rank and authority to get compliance. | 7. A leader uses influence to create the desire to follow the advice being given. |
| 8. An instructor considers the game, the activity, the program an end in itself. | 8. A leader uses activities as tools to teach attitudes and ideals. |
| 9. An instructor is content to work with those who come to the activity. | 9. A leader is concerned about those who don't come, and does something about it. |

from the instructor column than the leader, stop and adjust your actions.

What can you do to cultivate influence and become a leader? The list is endless. There are some basic things that most successful leaders have used to develop influence with those they work with. Review the items below carefully. Each one is considered an important component in leadership development.

# Goals

Be sure to set definite goals *with* your followers, and not *for* your followers. Always keep the goals in mind, and take action to achieve them. Nothing is more convincing than success. Goals should be used as the outline for a plan of action for the group. Never change the goals the group has set, unless requested to do so by the group members. If changes are necessary, plant the seeds of change with the followers. You must try to lead from behind with timely, tactful suggestions. Group members often accept new ideas quicker if they feel they, rather than the leader, generated the ideas.

# Direction

You must not only help the group set goals, but also help them determine the direction of these goals. In most cases, your goals should be agreeable to the group, as well as the organization the group belongs to. If they are not agreeable to the organization or society, you and the group members must be ready to accept the consequences of your actions. That means that you will need to consider your actions carefully. It is important not to make emotional decisions. First, you must plan your work, and then work your plan. Be adaptable and flexible, but never lose sight of your goals and continually move toward them. Create conditions favorable to your goals.

Providing direction means making decisions. People will not follow someone who cannot make decisions. Indecision confuses and frustrates people. Followers need to know where they are going and why. Don't let fear of making a wrong decision stop you from being a leader. Everyone makes mistakes, and it is important that you learn from your mistakes and make better decisions in the future.

The direction of the group will also be affected by the organizational skills of the leader. Prepare and study in advance for the activities and events that the group may engage in. You may have to seek the help of other group members to organize an important event. Leadership doesn't mean doing everything yourself. It is important for a leader to recognize there will always be something new to learn. You cannot grow and develop if you are not willing to learn about yourself, or investigate new ideas and methods. Take advantage of formal training opportunities to ensure you are as up-to-date as possible.

## Positive Attitude

To work toward your goals, you must develop a positive attitude. Leadership is an opportunity for service. You must radiate faith in your goals, purposes, and directions in your plans, programs, and actions. A positive attitude is contagious. Persevere in the face of obstacles and defeats, and encourage your followers to work through frustrations and disenchantments. An optimistic person can turn problems into opportunities. Spark ideas and try to cause good things to happen through others. Carefully watch the idea, and nourish it with help whenever and wherever needed. A leader should analyze failures and mistakes and learn from them. Mistakes can be turned into assets.

As a leader you must retain a professional manner with all of your followers. Although it is very difficult at times not to lose control, such an outburst can damage your position with group members. You also must learn to be tolerant of others. Not everyone has the same beliefs, customs, or values. You can learn a great deal from other people if you keep an open mind. Everyone has something to contribute to the group, and it is up to you as the leader to find each person's strengths.

## Honesty

Your honesty is of the utmost importance, although you may have to confess occasionally to a "setback" or a slight change of plans. You should never have an ulterior motive or keep a goal secret from your followers. Try to remain objective.

# Dare Yourself

You should try in your own way and to the best of your ability, to dare to do the unusual. True leaders are willing to take risks. Look around you and see how others dare to be different. Dare to be:

*An explorer, chart new courses, be an innovator, be a pioneer.*
*An originator, a problem solver.*
*A developer of new ideas, methods, and systems.*
*An inspiration to others. Move others to action.*

# Improve Conditions

This is one of the main duties of a leader. You should learn to respect group members as individuals and to be seriously interested in each one. Most successful leaders care about others. Remember that you are dealing with emotional human beings, not blocks of wood. Be concerned with their welfare, and when appropriate try to help them solve their personal problems. Strive to be a role model for group members. Walt Disney was a good example of someone who cared about the people who worked for him. He always took time to talk to the Disney employees about their families and problems. He took time to get to know people as individuals rather than just employees.

# Start Where They Are

It is important that your followers feel that you are one of them. You have to know their customs and how to speak their language. Listening to their music, watching their favorite television shows, and participating in their recreational events are a few ways to start where your followers are.

Follow up with people who drop out of the group. Try to find out why they are no longer active and if possible correct that condition. Create a group atmosphere where anyone will feel welcome to join. Seek and promote the talents of individual members.

# Heroes, Interests, Skills

Build on heroes, interests, and skills. Always lead them upward by easy steps to where they want to be. Your pace should not be any faster than the interest of the group suggests, and the slowest of the group can follow. Raise their egos and give them a place to shine. Recognize individuals and their progress. People need to feel good about themselves and have successes in their lives. Build on each person's skills. Work from their strengths rather than their weaknesses.

# Praise

People like to be praised, especially in front of others. Praise is one of the most important techniques a leader can use. People do not like to be ignored, and youngsters who do not get attention for the right things they do will do wrong things to get noticed. Praise your followers often but only when it is deserved. Flattery fails. The most effective praise is given in the hearing of others, or at a gathering of peers. When a person fails, you should give him a task in which he can succeed, and then praise him for it. Everyone needs the thrill of success. This story illustrates the power of praise.

David was an uncoordinated little boy who felt he never did anything right, who never completed a project, was a slow learner, a poor reader, and was always at the bottom of the class. He was seven years old and the butt of the other children's jokes. He was pushed around and picked on by most everybody until one day his world changed. His teacher gave him a gold star for being the best in the class. He raced home to show it to his mother.

"Look, Mom! I got a gold star from the teacher for being the best in the class. "You got a gold star," echoed his unbelieving mother, "What were you the best in?" she asked. "It was in singing class and the teacher said that we should open our mouths wide, and I opened mine the widest." David said proudly.

For once in his life his ego was very high, and his frustration low. He thought his teacher was wonderful, and wasn't she? She had been looking for a long time for something about David that she could praise. A tiny skill, and a clever teacher. Don't overlook a chance to praise, it can do wonderful things.

# Train Followers to Lead

How can you do all the things a leader ought to do all alone? It seems too big an order for one person, especially an inexperienced new leader. One way to solve your problem is to train others in the group to lead. Always be on the alert to find potential leaders among the group. Watch out for the dominant ones in the group. Create opportunities for them to do good for others, to make choices, take responsibilities, and exercise and develop leadership. Don't offer them too many decisions to make or too many responsibilities at first. If possible, put them into situations where they succeed early. If they fail, help them to learn from it and try again. Invent situations where they can be applauded. See that they understand the goals of the group and the program. Develop a leadership program that allows a person to progress to higher duties and responsibilities. Badges, emblems, pins, certificates, graduations, and trips can be used for special recognition. Give credit freely but only where it is deserved.

# Network with Others

Cooperation and assistance from your followers or others outside the group are important for the group's success. Neither you nor your group can exist without the help of others. You can get cooperation by achieving goals, by earning it, being worthy of it, and by giving it. The Boys' Club director in the example below earned cooperation from the local merchants.

The new Boys' Club in a small town was getting little support from the local businesses in the community. Several of the merchants were even antagonistic toward the club. One day the director of the Boys' Club learned that the merchants were sponsoring a festival and a boxing exhibition had been planned. He called on the festival coordinator and offered to set up his portable boxing ring and have his experienced boxing instructor and referee present at the event. He also offered to help in any other way the committee wanted. After the festival, the Boys' Club never had opposition again from the merchants.

Get to know other leaders and learn from them. Observation is one way to learn and improve your leadership skills. It is O.K. to adopt other people's ideas to your group. When necessary, modify the ideas to meet the need for your group. However, sharing is a a two-way street. Be sure to share your successes with others. They can learn from your experiences. Also, don't hesitate to contact and enlist the help of commercial organizations in your efforts.

## Safety

The safety of your followers must be uppermost in your mind and that of your followers. Avoid hazards and dangers by preparing against them. Train your followers in safety measures and develop a risk management plan.

## Keep the Group Together

Always be aware of possible cleavages in the group. As a leader you should expect to handle conflict. Win the cooperation of probable ringleaders and other influential members by including them in your planning process. Create activities that will give them an opportunity to shine, get applause, and be recognized.

As you review this list, don't get discouraged if you don't feel like you know how to handle conflict, set goals and direction, train others, give praise or how to do any of the other items listed above. Remember leadership is a set of skills that can be learned. You can learn how to be a leader through **observation, practice, and training.** Many organizations that provide leadership opportunities also provide training for their leaders. People are not born to be leaders. Leadership skills and influence are developed. A leader never stops learning.

# Program LeadershipTechniques

As a leader you may have an opportunity to organize programs for special groups. Program ideas are many and varied, but these tried and true leadership hints listed below may help you in your planning efforts. These techniques can be used in conjunction with the techniques already discussed. Additional leadership techniques for leading special groups will be presented in Chapter Four.

1. Challenge your followers to something new and different, things not easy to learn. People get bored and lose interest if they are not introduced to new challenges. Everyone needs to be stretched beyond their comfort zone from time to time in order to grow. It is no disgrace if they fail.

2. Use their ideas whenever practical. Encourage group members to share their ideas with you. As the leader you should recognize good ideas from others and support their development.

3. Build programs on their questions. Don't always answer their questions. Say "Let's find out!" Learning by doing is a wonderful way to learn. Never short-circuit experience. Don't make it easy for them by giving answers or solutions to problems. Let them find out for themselves. The procedures, the process, the journey, and the experience are most important. Do not do for them what they can do for themselves. Let them learn from their mistakes under your guidance.

4. Learn their interests and skills and build programs on these.

5. Anticipation should be created and fostered by painting word pictures, displaying posters, and distributing articles in advance that describe sights, places, events, and people to be involved in the program. Whet their appetites. A leader should create enthusiasm.

6. Time must be made available for you to listen to your followers, to consult, think, organize, and plan with them and receive their ideas. Organize your time well. Never be caught up with trivia or doing what others can do.

7.  Interest and fun should accompany educational, vocational, and other more technical subjects.  Hard work and learning can be fun.
8.  Introduce color, drama, and glamour into every program where possible.  Make your programs exciting.  People enjoy novelty, surprise, change, risk, adventure, and challenge.
9.  Food is magic!  Include it as often as possible.  Food can be used to set the mood of a party or entice the outsider to come in and participate.

# Leadership Words

To end this chapter, make a list of all the leadership phrases you can use to gain influence.  The following phrases are just a start:

"Please ..."
"If you don't mind ..."
"I'd like you to ..."
"I'm proud of you because ..."
"Have you thought about..."
"What do the others think about ..."
"Can you find the time to..."
"Have you the energy ..."
"I need someone strong.  Can you ..."
"You have a lot of enthusiasm.  Maybe you can ..."
"How would you like to ...?"
"That is excellent!  Now, how about ..."
"How do the others feel about ...?"
"What do you say to ...?"
"Have you considered ...?"
"Let's ..."

Now you can add to this list.  I wish you success as a leader. Review this chapter as often as needed.  Becoming a leader will take practice so expect to make mistakes in the early years of your journey into leadership.  Each leadership situation will be different and will require you to use new and different leadership skills. You will never be able to stop learning. The next chapters have been designed to introduce you to other techniques that will help you become a successful leader.

# 4

# Leading Special Groups

In the previous chapters the basic skills of effective leadership were discussed. While these skills provide a firm foundation for leadership, they do not address the many skills that are needed to lead special groupings of people such as children, older adults, the gifted, or the economically disadvantaged. A leader of a special group will not be successful unless the unique needs and behaviors of the group participants are understood. This chapter highlights the leadership techniques that can be used with four special groups; children, older adults, the disabled, and the economically disadvantaged. If you decide to work extensively with one of these groups, you should supplement your leadership training with additional readings and on-the-job experiences.

## Leading People Grouped by Age

When working with any group of people, it is important to recognize that people pass through various stages of growth and development. You should be aware of these stages and the different needs of people during them. Life stages include the time periods of infancy, early childhood, middle childhood, adolescence, young adulthood, middle adulthood, and older adulthood. The emphasis in this chapter will be on leadership techniques to use with children in the middle childhood (6-12 years old), and adolescence stages (13-19 years old), and with adults in the older adulthood stage (over 60).

## Leading children

Leading children of any age is challenging. During childhood, motor skills, social skills, beliefs, values, self-confidence, self-esteem and other life skills are developed. Children need to be nurtured by parents, teachers, and leaders. Programs need to be developed that allow children to develop the appropriate life skills. Learning experiences should be provided that stretch an individual physically, mentally, and emotionally. If you are working with a group in which some of the participants have higher levels of ability than others, occasionally group the participants according to their abilities or talents. By allowing the advanced participants to work together or to attend special programs, they can expand their abilities. Make every effort to encourage creativity in your group members. Do not expect everyone to conform. Children need to express their individuality and develop special talents. However, this does not mean that group members should be disruptive or infringe on the rights of others. Children also need to learn to compromise, share, and work with other group members on projects. You should respect and value each child's contribution to the group. As you work with a group, strive to develop an atmosphere of openness and mutual respect.

A key to successful leadership with children of any age is to understand the developmental characteristics of the various age groups. If you understand the needs of each group you can modify your leadership style to try to meet those needs. Children ages 6 to 19 are usually put into four segments: 6 to 8, 9 to 11, 12 to 14, and 15 to 19. The developmental characteristics of children and the implications for leadership are outlined below. (This material is adapted from Developmental Characteristics of the 4-H Member, by Ann Y. Frazier, Extension 4-H Specialist, North Carolina Agricultural Extension Service, 1986.)

There are two major leadership approaches you can take when working with children. One is called pedagogy—learning through a teacher—and the other is a helping or self-directed leadership approach called andragogy. As Edginton and Ford [1985] point out, these terms should be viewed on a leadership style continuum and not as an either/or situation. The leadership style you use should vary along this continuum. Factors such as

# Developmental Characteristics of Youth

## Six to Eight Age Group

| Characteristics | Leadership Implications |
|---|---|
| 1. Easily motivated, eager to try something new. | 1. Plan a wide variety of activities. |
| 2. Sensitive to criticism, doesn't accept failure well. Frustration comes quickly. | 2. Plan activities that take a short time to complete. |
| 3. Experimental, exploratory behavior part of development. | 2. Provide positive encouragement and help. |
| 4. Learns best if physically active. | 2. Plan activities in which success can be experienced. |
| 5. Strong desire for affection and attention of adults. | 2. Set up situations with minimum competition. |
| 6. Limited attention span (15-20 minutes). | 3. Provide opportunities for hands-on experiences. |
|  | 4. Provide opportunities for physical action. |
| 7. Needs to repeat activities that are well known and mastered. | 5. Plan for small group activities with an adult for each three to four children. |
| 8. Begins to test independence. | 6., 7. Provide a variety of short and specific learning activities. |
|  | 8. Allow the group to decide some of the activities they want planned. |

## Nine to Eleven Age Group

| Characteristics | Leadership Implications |
|---|---|
| 1. Are quite active, with boundless energy. | 1. Place emphasis on active learning experiences. |
| 2. Like group activities. | 2. Emphasize group learning experiences. |
| 3. Like to be with members of their own sex. | 3. Encourage working in groups with members of the same sex. |
| 4. Have interests which often change rapidly, jumping from one thing to another. | 4. Plan a variety of short group activities. |
| 5. Idolization of significant others – hero worship. | 5. Encourage apprenticing with older youth and other adults. |
| 6. Beginning to accept responsibility for self and others. | 6. Let the group members plan an activity. |
| 7. Are easily motivated, eager to try something new. Willingness to seek risk and adventure. | 7. Challenge the group with new and different experiences. Encourage them to ask questions. |
| 8. Need guidance from adults to stay at a task and to achieve their best performance. High need for skill development. | 8. Work closely with the group members to encourage completion of work. |

## Twelve to Fourteen Age Group

| Characteristics | Leadership Implications |
| --- | --- |
| 1. Are concerned about physical development, acceptance by friends, social graces and good grooming. | 1. Encourage learning activities related to understanding yourself and getting along with others. |
| 2. Group affiliation is important. | 2. Provide opportunity for leadership in a group setting. |
| 3. Continued development of independence yet wants and needs adult help. | 3. Encourage working with adults and older teens. |
| 4. Seeking self-identity. Are self-conscious, with many needing help for inferiority complexes. | 4. Concentrate on developing individual skills. |
| 5. Interested in fan clubs, with many having adult idols. | 5. Encourage work with adults and older teens to complete projects. |
| 6. Are interested in members of the opposite sex. Are interested in activities involving boys and girls. | 6. Encourage learning experiences involving boys and girls. |
| 7. Are interested in sports and active games. | 7. Encourage active, fun oriented activities. |
| 8. Are ready for in-depth, longer learning experiences. | 8. Allow the youth to take more responsibility for planning group activities. |
| 9. Are getting over the age of fantasy and beginning to think of what they will do when they grow up, but are often unclear of need and values. | 9. Provide opportunities to relate leadership life skills to career choices. |

## Fifteen to Nineteen Age Group

| Characteristics | Leadership Implications |
| --- | --- |
| 1. Have social needs and desires that are strong. | 1. Emphasize leadership life skills that also relate to social development. |
| 2. Want and need a strong voice in planning their own program. | 2. Allow members to plan programs with the guidance and support of adults. |
| 3. Want adult leadership roles. | 3. Encourage working with adult leaders. |
| 4. Are interested in co-educational activities. | 4. Encourage co-educational learning experiences. |
| 5. Have areas of interest that are more consistent. | 5. Encourage greater in-depth study of leadership roles and life skills. |
| 6. Are developing a community consciousness. | 6. Encourage learning activities involving the community. |
| 7. Potential for high alienation from family, adults, and society. | 7. Promote open communication between teens and adults. |
| 8. Full development of physique and physical powers. | 8. Apply leadership life skills to problem solving and decision making. |
| 9. Team and group allegiance important. | 9. Encourage group participation as well as individual skill development. |

the maturity of the children in the group, their levels of self-motivation, experience, and their need for extrinsic and intrinsic rewards should be considered when selecting a leadership style. In general, the younger the children, the more pedagogical the leader's approach should be. A lack of maturity, limited experiences, and a stronger need for extrinsic rewards is usually exhibited by younger children, and requires the leader to assume a teaching role more often than a facilitating role. However, when working with teenagers, a leader should try to vary the leadership style. Although some teenagers can often appear immature and dependent upon others, they also have a need to express their independence and show a greater need for intrinsic rewards. When appropriate, a good leader will relinquish the role of teacher and become the facilitator for the group. Group members should be actively involved in making decisions, setting goals, and planning group activities. Instead of planning a weekend retreat for teens, allow them to plan the retreat themselves. The experience the teens will gain from participating in a self-directed program will give them a chance to develop needed life skills.

Providing new leadership opportunities for teenagers is one way of allowing them to be self-directed. Using teens as teachers, peer counselors, and agency advocates allows them to become involved in experiences designed to strengthen their self-esteem and confidence. With training and adult guidance, teens can assume leadership roles beyond the traditional ones of holding an office or serving on a committee. Young children look up to older teens, and are influenced by them. School officials, health agency directors, and youth directors have found that teens can be more effective than adults in dealing with children about drugs, alcohol abuse, and other youth issues. For a self-directed teen leadership program to succeed, the adults affiliated with the program have to believe that teenagers can perform successfully in the roles of teacher, counselor, and advocate. You should also foster an environment that encourages success. For teenagers, that means giving them adult leadership roles, but also providing adult support and guidance. Teen leadership programs such as Teens Reaching Youth (TRY) sponsored by the North Carolina 4-H program, provide teenagers an opportunity to teach under the guidance of an adult coach. The teens teach in teams of two. Each team must have an adult coach who provides guidance, encouragement, and feedback to the team members about their teaching, but is not actively involved in the teaching process. The TRY teams attend statewide or regional training sessions to learn teaching techniques, how to work with children, how to develop a lesson plan, and additional subject matter that they can teach. To strengthen the commitment to the teaching experience, each team signs a contract committing to teach an agreed number of groups. The whole experience is designed to place the teenager in a position that will require him to learn new skills, and assume some responsibilities, yet allow him to call on the coach for help and guidance.

As a leader you will have the responsibility of helping youth to acquire knowledge and skills in a variety of activities. Learning can involve acquiring specific knowledge or skills in a subject such as nutrition or soil science, or it can involve developing beliefs and values. In order for learning to take place, certain elements need to be present in the environment. These elements are meaningfulness, supportive social climate, noncoercive participation, and effective communication [Edginton and Ford, 1985].

## Meaningfulness

A child will be motivated to learn if he feels the learning situation is important. To ensure that your learning experiences are individually meaningful, base your instruction on the experience, skill level, and perceptions of the participants. When possible, involve group members in planning the activities.

## Supportive social climate

It is important that group members are provided with a positive climate in which to learn. You should be concerned with the development of each group member. Encouragement and support from you and other group members is important. Treat all children with respect and dignity.

## Noncoercive participation

Learning takes place more freely in a situation where participation is voluntary. Design programs and experiences that will allow children to participate freely. If children can choose to participate in activities rather than being coerced, they will have a more enjoyable and satisfying experience.

### Effective communication

An instructional leader must realize that in order to be effective, two-way communication must be established with group members. The teacher cannot simply teach. The participants must feel free to ask questions and express their opinions. Selection of the appropriate teaching techniques is also important. You should consider the type of knowledge, skills, or values you are trying to teach. For example, if you are teaching teenagers problem solving, role-playing is an instructional technique that could be used. If you were going to teach an activity such as sewing, demonstration would be an appropriate technique to facilitate learning. The age, skill level, and expertise of the group members must also be considered when selecting teaching techniques.

In summary, leading children is exciting, challenging, and demanding. You must have understanding, unlimited patience, enthusiasm, flexibility, and confidence. As a leader, you must be aware of the developmental characteristics of the age group you are working with, and facilitate the appropriate physical, mental, and emotional development. Creativity and self-expression need to be encouraged. Your leadership style should shift along the continuum of teacher to helper to meet the needs of the group. Factors such as the maturity of the group members, their level of motivation, and their life experiences should influence your selection of a leadership style. If you are able to create a learning environment that is meaningful, positive and encouraging, that allows for participation without coercion, and also promotes communication, the opportunity for learning is greatly enhanced.

# Leading Older Adults

Leading older adults is no different from leading any other group of adults. They have the same need for recognition, creativity, special interaction, expansion of knowledge and skills, and involvement as anyone else. Don't let stereotypes about older people limit your effectiveness with this important group.

You must realize that aging is very individual and variable. Although older people may experience a decline in health, they are not all ill or handicapped. Many prefer active rather than sedentary activities. The term "older adult" also represents several age groups. A group of adults ranging in age from 60 to 100 represents more than one generation. The saying, "You can't teach an old dog new tricks" should not be applied to older adults. They can learn new things, and most have a desire to remain self-directive. As with any life stage, entering older adulthood does mean change for an individual. During this period, people must adjust to retirement, reduced mobility, possibly the loss of a spouse and/or friends, and changes in health. You must be sensitive to these events, and help group members make the necessary adjustments. However, regardless of the life changes that are made, you should remember that older people are no different from other people; they just happen to be a little older.

Although leadership techniques used with older adults are the same as those for other age groups, the following guidelines and techniques might be helpful when working with older adults.

1.  Treat older people as adults. Many people think just because a person is old, he must be senile, which is untrue. Older adults expect to be treated with respect and dignity. They have experiences and knowledge they can share with others. To do less will affect their feelings of dignity and self-worth.
2.  Avoid stereotyping older people. Most older adults will contradict the stereotypes and myths.
3.  Recognize the unique skills and experiences of each group member. Each person can contribute to the group. You will find that the group will respond to you if you are interested in their needs and desires.
4.  Act as a facilitator, rather than a teacher to the group whenever possible. Encourage the group members to plan, organize, and carry out their own activities. You should not interact in a superior-subordinate manner with group members.
5.  Avoid talking loudly and over-articulating your words. Not all older adults are hard-of-hearing. You do not

want to appear to the group as if you are talking down to
them.

6. Some older adults experience hearing loss and visual
problems. It is important to be sensitive to these problems.
Use of large print reading material and elimination of
unnecessary background noise may help improve
communication.

7. Avoid suggesting activities and programs that are not
age-appropriate for the group. Programs should match
the interest and sophistication of the group.

8. When planning events, be sensitive to the dietary
restrictions and financial limitations of participants. Many
may follow low-sugar and no-salt diets and may live on
fixed incomes.

The leadership skills and techniques that you will use with
specific participant age groupings should be governed in part by
the life development stage of the group members. Understanding
the needs and desires of each age group is critical to successful
leadership. Children and adults both respond to leaders who are
concerned with their needs, interests, and desires. It is important
that you use techniques that will build a relationship of trust and
openness among group members and also between yourself and
group members.

# Leading People Grouped by Special Circumstances

## Leading people with disabilities

As a leader you may find yourself working with people who
have disabilities. In addition to understanding their needs from
a lifespan development aspect, you must also understand their
needs as they relate to the disability. Edginton and Ford [1985]
define disability as a condition that has a potential to limit major
life activities. As a leader, you must realize that disabilities exist
on a continuum. Some disabilities may have little or no impact
on an individual's lifestyle and others have a major impact.
There are five categories of disabilities: the physically disabled,
the psychologically disabled, the visually impaired, the hearing
impaired, and the developmentally disabled. Each of these

categories has a range of functioning levels and associated conditions. Although a discussion of these disabilities is beyond the scope of this book, you are encouraged to learn more about a specific disability through additional reading.

While specific leadership techniques will not be outlined for each disability, a general list of techniques that can be used by a leader in a community setting is presented below.    These techniques can be used in the situation in which the disabled person joins a group of non-disabled people. If you elect to work exclusively with people who have a specific disability, you will need additional training concerning the leadership techniques appropriate for that group.

1.   Use common sense.  Ask the disabled group member what type of help is preferred.  Assist the person only when asked. A person will ask for help when it is needed.
2.   Treat the disabled member just like you treat everyone else in the group.  Accept the person as an individual who has the same basic needs and desires as other people.  He or she can participate in a wide range of activities.
3.   Have a positive attitude toward the person.  You are a role model for the other group members.  Your actions will influence how the rest of the group will react to the disabled member [Edginton and Ford, 1985].
4.   Try to eliminate barriers and conditions that may hinder the disabled member from participating in group activities. Make activity modifications and improvise when necessary.
5.   Treat disabled people in an age-appropriate manner. Disabled adults should be treated as adults.
6.   Recognize that the disabled group member may need extra time to complete tasks and plan accordingly.
7.   Relax, be yourself, and have fun.  Don't try to be overly friendly or pious.  Interact with the disabled group member just as you would with other group members.

The techniques listed above, together with the general leadership skills previously discussed in earlier chapters, provide a framework for effective leadership with the disabled.  As a leader, your major role is to help the disabled person to become integrated into the group.  People with disabilities are people who happen to have a condition that may affect their level of activity. They need an opportunity to become a contributing member of a group.

## Leading the economically disadvantaged

The economically disadvantaged are the portion of our population that live in poverty. Poverty means more than not having enough money. It means limited access to education, housing and medical care, inadequate nutrition, and low self-esteem. Leaders who work with the economically disadvantaged have to be concerned with the whole person. They must be prepared to deal with the social issues that impact on people and lead to frustrations. The most successful leaders who work with the economically disadvantaged are members of that group rather than outsiders. The successful 4-H clubs, Boy Scout troops and other youth groups located in housing projects are the ones that are organized and led by people who live in the housing projects. The leaders were specifically recruited from the area and trained to work with children in their neighborhood. Leading the economically disadvantaged is not easy whether you are dealing with children or adults. While general leadership techniques can be used with this group, there are other techniques that will help the leader in working with the economically deprived.

1.  Understand their lifestyle. Do not attempt to judge their actions. You want to be perceived as a friend, and someone who cares about them.
2.  Plan activities in which they are interested. Let them decide what they want to do and help in the planning of the activity. Plan activities that are designed to build life skills and self-esteem.
3.  Give them as much responsibility as they can handle. Provide for recognition and praise for accomplishments. Watch for leaders within the group and put them in charge. Give them the skills to solve their own problems.
4.  Network with their organizations and use their leaders as much as possible.

5.  Make use of the various outside resources and services that could assist the group. You cannot work alone.
6.  Encourage group members to accomplish things for themselves and solve their own problems. Allowing people to help themselves can increase their motivation and improve their self-esteem.
7.  Prepare group members for new social and cultural experiences. Make sure they know how to act appropriately. If members are embarrassed or feel uncomfortable, the beneficial learning experience will do more harm than good.

In this chapter, additional leadership techniques have been presented that can be used when working with special groups. Your success as a leader will come from your ability to meet the needs of your group participants. Children, older adults, the disabled, and the economically deprived are people who have different needs, interests, desires, and abilities. An understanding of life stage development is essential to effective leadership. It is important that you do not limit your perceptions of any special group because of a belief in myths and stereotypes about the group. As a leader, you must be objective and serve as a role model for the other group members. Using the general leadership skills presented in earlier chapters and the special techniques presented here, you can provide effective leadership for your group members.

# 5

# Time Management

Being a good leader means more than learning leadership skills. You must also have organizational skills. One of the most important organizational skills in successful leadership is time management. For many, the acceptance of a leadership position means an additional commitment of time and energy in an already busy schedule. If the leader, the agency, and the participants are to gain maximum benefit from the experience, the leader should know how to get the most out of a 24-hour day. Remember, time is a unique resource. You can manage time but you cannot save it. What you don't use is gone forever!

## How to Get Organized

One of the first steps in time management is getting organized. You cannot be successful unless you establish goals and prioritize work. Being organized takes time, and you may think that you don't have enough time to get organized. But if you stop and think about it, the reason you don't have time may be that you are not organized. You have the same 24 hours as everyone else. Being well organized will give you more time in your life as well as reduce stress, increase your productivity, and allow you to retain control of your life. To determine how organized you are, take the quiz developed by Stephanie Culp [1986].

## What's your organization I.Q.?

To find out how organized you are, answer the following questions YES or NO.

1.  Have you reached the point where you find yourself deliberately not opening the mail for days at a time?

    YES _____    NO _____

2.  Does the top of your desk look like the national archives? Is it so cluttered with piles of paper that you don't have any space left to do your work?

    YES _____    NO _____

3.  Do you tell everyone around you not to touch a thing on your desk, because in spite of the apparent mess, you know exactly where everything is?

    YES _____    NO _____

4.  Has your telephone, electricity, or other utility been turned off, or have your credit cards been stopped, simply because you never have the time to pay the bills, return their calls or answer their letters?

    YES _____    NO _____

5.  Are some of your friends and relatives annoyed because you never have the time to return their calls or answer their letters?

    YES _____    NO _____

6.  Do you keep piles of newspapers and magazines you haven't read because there's something very important that you must read in each paper or magazine? You simply have to read it all, but so far, you haven't had the time to do so?

    YES _____    NO _____

7.  Does your hall closet remind you of Fibber McGee? Did the pots and pans stage an outright revolt the last time you opened your kitchen cupboard?

    YES _____    NO _____

8.  Do you have piles of things in your house or office – are things stuffed under the bed, stacked in boxes, or packed in bags, all waiting for the day when you have the time to go through everything and then figure out where to put it? You keep telling yourself if only ... if only I had the time ... if only I had more closet space.

    YES _____    NO _____

9.  Is your garage so full that there's no room for the car?

    YES _____    NO _____

10. Do you find yourself avoiding phone calls and socializing because you just don't have the time to deal with people, or just don't feel like dealing with them?

    YES _____    NO _____

11. Do you often have a problem figuring out what clothes to wear even though your closet is full of clothes?
    YES _____    NO _____

12. Does your day usually start with a crisis, and get worse from there?
    YES _____    NO _____

13. Do you have a difficult time making decisions, and because of that, often put off making the decision until the situation becomes an emergency?
    YES _____    NO _____

14. Are you very particular about how things are done, and how they look?
    YES _____    NO _____

15. Do you have so many "to do" lists that you don't know where to begin?
    YES _____    NO _____

16. Do you feel uncomfortable about hiring others to do things for you, since you are certain that they will not be able to do the job properly, and because of that, you might as well do it yourself?
    YES _____    NO _____

17. Do you have trouble finding enough time for all areas in your life – work, leisure, family, and spiritual needs, plus some private time for yourself?
    YES _____    NO _____

18. Do you forget important dates, such as anniversaries and birthdays?
    YES _____    NO _____

19. Do you think that perfectionism is the same as excellence?
    YES _____    NO _____

20. Are you constantly plagued by interruptions from others and as a result never seem to get anything done?
    YES _____    NO _____

21. Have you given up trying to balance your checkbook but at the same time you haven't given it to a professional so that it can be balanced for you?
    YES _____    NO _____

22. Do you have some kind of legal or accounting problem pending that could have been avoided if you had been more organized?
    YES _____    NO _____

23. Do you often want to stay in bed instead of getting up to face yet another chaotic day?
    YES _____    NO _____

24. Have you missed a promotion, a sale, or an opportunity of some kind because you didn't have the time to get organized so that you could make a proper presentation?
    YES _____    NO _____

25.    Do you often find yourself agreeing to do something just because you didn't know how to say no, and as a result you spend an inordinate amount of time trying to get out of the obligation?

YES _____        NO _____

26.    Is the clutter in your life so overwhelming that you don't know where to begin to sort it all out?

YES _____        NO _____

**SCORING:**
Each YES answer is worth one point. Your organizational score can be determined by adding all of your YES answers.

**IF YOUR SCORE IS**

1-6    Congratulations. You are relatively organized. You probably have good time management. You may find some useful tips in this chapter that you have not tried before.

7-12    You've got a little problem with time and/or organization. It's probably time to begin implementing some of the techniques outlined in this chapter.

12-15    If you feel as if you have totally lost control, chances are you have, or are about to. Your organizational problems are compounded by your apparent lack of time. Read this chapter carefully and begin on a program to regain control of your life.

15-26    You are so disorganized, you probably don't know if you are coming or going. Chaos is a way of life for you. Your life is running you, instead of you running your life. It's time for an organizational overhaul. (*How to Get Organized* ©1986 Stephanie Culp. Used by permission of Writer's Digest Books)

If your score is higher than 12, don't despair—the steps discussed next can help get your life under control.

# Steps to Organization

There are many techniques and methods that you can use to become better organized. The three steps discussed here provide practical suggestions but they do not ensure organization. Figure 5.1 outlines the steps in time management organization. There is

# Steps in Time Management Organization

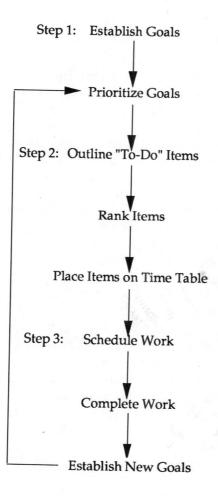

Step 1:    Establish Goals

Prioritize Goals

Step 2:  Outline "To-Do" Items

Rank Items

Place Items on Time Table

Step 3:    Schedule Work

Complete Work

Establish New Goals

Figure 5.1

no magic formula for becoming organized. As with the leadership techniques discussed earlier, the steps to organization must be practiced and adopted to your unique situation. You must want to get the most out of life before you can become organized. Once you realize how valuable your time is, it will be well worth the time and effort it takes to get organized.

### Establish goals

Without realistic and attainable goals, it is impossible to get organized. Goals provide purpose and direction for all aspects of life. We cannot spend our time wisely if we don't know where we are going or what we want to accomplish. Buy a notebook and begin writing down both your short- and long-term goals. Writing down goals will help ensure your commitment to them. Stephanie Culp pointed out in *How to Get Organized When You Don't Have Time* [1986] that recent studies show that the success rate of people who write down their goals is about ninety times greater than those who don't. Write down your goals and establish a deadline for each one. For example, one short-term goal you might have is "to acquire a volunteer position with the YMCA in six months." A long-term goal might be "to become the Coordinator of Volunteer Services at the YMCA in three years." Establishing goals is not a once in a lifetime experience. So, don't just write down your goals and then put them on the shelf. Periodically review them and make modifications. As you reach your goals, add new ones and revise old goals.

Once you have established your goals, you can begin to prioritize them. Some will be more important than others, so spend most of your time on those most important to you. If you are unable to set priorities, you will find yourself spending a lot of time on many jobs but never accomplishing anything.

### Outline "to-do" items

In order to achieve your goals, many smaller tasks have to be accomplished. For each goal, list the items you need to complete to reach the goal. You may have to divide some goals into smaller projects and then outline a "to-do" list for each project. The long-term goal of becoming the Coordinator of Volunteer Services at the YMCA provides a good example.

LONG-TERM GOAL:   Coordinator of Volunteer
                         Services – YMCA
                         Deadline: three years

Project 1:   Acquire an entry-level volunteer
                         position at the YMCA
                         Deadline: six months.

"To-Do" List:
- Obtain a volunteer application from YMCA
- Research volunteer positions available
- Make an appointment with Volunteer Coordinator
- Interview with appropriate staff
- Attend in-service training

Project 2:   Coordinate Summer Day Camp – YMCA
                         Deadline: two years

"To-Do" List:
- Meet with staff to discuss summer schedule
- Recruit four volunteers to help with camp
- Design summer camp flier
- Mail flier to youth members
- Purchase arts and craft supplies
- Train volunteers working with camp
- Register campers

Project 3:   Continuing Education Classes
                         Deadline: six months to one year

"To-Do" List:
- Obtain information on educational opportunities
- Enroll in management classes
- Attend annual seminar on volunteer management

Rank projects and the items on the "to-do" list and place them on a time table. Revise your list as needed. Check off each item as it is accomplished. You will feel great as you see your list become smaller and smaller.

### Schedule your work

Once you have outlined all the things you must do, schedule your time appropriately. Purchase an appointment book in which you can record daily, weekly, and monthly schedules. There are many "Week-at-a-Glance" and "Day-at-a-Glance" calendar books available at stationery stores. More sophisticated planning systems are also available. These systems are more expensive than a calendar, but provide a complete planning package including sections for goals, projects, and scheduling. Review several of the systems and select the one that meets your needs. What is most important is that you begin to schedule your time. Don't rely on your memory. Dates and activities can easily be forgotten when you are busy. An appointment book can also help you control your time. It is important that you build flexibility into your schedule. Try to leave some unbooked time that can be used in case of delays or unforeseen schedule changes. As you look at your schedule, make sure that you don't overschedule the "to-dos." Set aside time for yourself – personal time is just as important as the time you give to others. Strive for a balance in your life between work, play, family, and yourself. It is necessary to enjoy life.

As you work to organize your life, don't get discouraged if from time to time you fall back into some of your old habits. Everyone wastes time. Procrastination is difficult to avoid. When you find yourself procrastinating, admit that you are wasting time. Examine the situation to find out why you are wasting time, and then try to eliminate the problem.

# Time Management

Aside from becoming organized, there are two other actions you can take to manage your time more efficiently. One is to plan your time. The idea of planning your time goes beyond putting dates in an appointment book. You plan for success rather than simply letting things happen. It means identifying and setting priorities for all your activities. Planning means scheduling time for thinking and reflection. Recognize your productive hours. If you are a morning person, use that time to tackle top priority tasks and leave low-priority tasks for the less productive hours. You also need to learn to delegate tasks to others. You don't have to do everything yourself. In general, you should not do anything that could be delegated to someone else. Delegation should not be limited to the work place, you can delegate personal chores also. If possible, hire a cleaning service to clean your house, take your car to a car wash, or send some of your laundry to a professional laundry.

Another key to effective time management is avoiding procrastination. Everyone is sometimes guilty of putting off things until a later date. While a little procrastination is not harmful, failure to act in a timely manner can create crises for you and others affected by your action. The three major causes of procrastination are unpleasant tasks to perform, difficult projects, and perfectionism.

If you find that you keep postponing a project because it is unpleasant, there are several tactics to try. Promise yourself a reward for completing the task, which can act as a motivator. You might sit down and finish your long-range plan if you know you can go for a walk in the park upon its completion. Be sure to take your reward if you reach your goal. You earned it. You can also try scheduling the unpleasant task first on your "to do" list rather than leaving it until last. By doing this you can get the task behind you and move on to other more exciting activities. Avoiding the task will not make it go away. If you are working with other people who have a problem with procrastination, try setting deadlines for them. The deadline imposed by a superior may be just enough to spark action.

When you are faced with a project that seems insurmountable, rather than procrastinating, try breaking the project down into manageable tasks. Plan mini-jobs that can be completed in 5 or 10 minutes to get you started. As you complete the smaller tasks, the impossible project becomes possible. If you are trying to do something creative and you can't afford to wait for inspiration, force yourself to spend 30 minutes a day working on the project. Just do anything for the first few days even if you think you are wasting time. Soon the inspiration will come, and you will be spending hours on the project.

People who procrastinate a great deal tend to be perfectionists. They do not like to compromise, and believe that a project is not completed, unless everything is perfect. Perfectionists are usually plagued with indecision about a project. This is because they want to avoid risking failure. If you are a perfectionist, you should try to realize that you don't have to be perfect. You must make the best decisions you can based on the information at hand. Accept that if you make a wrong decision you can deal with it at a later date.

# Rules of Time Management

Getting the most from your time requires dedication and discipline. The following time management rules summarize the basic steps of time management. Whenever you feel like you just don't have time to do the things in life you want to do review these rules. They should help regain control of your time.

### Basic rules of time management

1. Understand the value of your time.
2. Plan your time. Plan for success.
3. Clarify your goals and establish priorities.
4. Make a list of things to do. Consolidate tasks.
5. Budget your time between work, leisure, family and yourself.
6. Be flexible.
7. Delegate tasks to others.
8. Learn to say no.
9. Avoid procrastination.
10. Recognize when you are wasting time and take corrective action.
11. Keep an appointment book or calendar.
12. Recognize your productive hours.

If you can learn to manage your time efficiently, you will be able to find the time to do the activities in your life that are important. Wise time management will also reduce stress, increase your productivity, and allow you to control your time. Managing your time will take practice and commitment. Becoming organized is probably the first major step in time management. Although there is no magic formula for becoming organized, the steps outlined in this chapter can provide some guidance. Find out which ones work for you. You cannot be an effective leader if you cannot handle difficult or unpleasant tasks in a timely fashion, so try to avoid procrastination. The basic rules of time management outlined above can serve as a guide. Now is the time to start getting your life organized. Leadership opportunities cannot be accepted if you cannot find the time.

# 6

# Volunteers are Wonderful

*"Volunteerism will continue to become more powerful, and will have increasing visibility, viability, importance and recognition in this country."*
*Eva Schindler Rainman [1988, p.16.6]*

Bobby Hill, a 13-year-old black boy in Waycross, Georgia, son of a U.S. Air Force sergeant, read about Dr. Schweitzer and his wonderful medical missionary work with the natives of Africa. There was a great need for medicine, and Bobby had an idea that he immediately put into action. He wrote his father's Commanding Officer, Lt. Gen. Richard C. Lindsay at NATO Headquarters in Naples, Italy, saying that he wanted very much to send some medicine to help Dr. Schweitzer, but that he didn't know how to get it there. Continuing his letter he said, "I asked my father to buy some medicine with my allowance money and send it to Dr. Schweitzer. Since I found no other way, I thought that if any of your airplanes fly where Dr. Schweitzer is, maybe they would deliver it for me. Some other people may want to give medicine too, because I read that a whole lot is needed by the people."

The general turned this appeal over to a local Italian radio station, and after it was read on the air, contributions poured in from all over Italy. All in all, $40,000 worth of medicine (9,000 pounds) was collected, and sure enough, one of the general's planes did "fly that way" and delivered the whole load to Dr. Schweitzer. Arrangements were made for the boy to accompany the gift to the famed missionary hospital.

Just an example of one person with a fine idea and the initiative to put the idea into action. Bobby was a volunteer.

Have you an idea that should be translated into action? Is there a need in your community that you might help meet? With the help of others, you are much more powerful than you think. One match can light up 10,000 others. You can be that match. Volunteering is just one way you can become a leader.

If you have the feeling that you can't do very much, you are wrong. You can do a lot. You can be very important. It only took one concerned person to start youth organizations such as the Boy Scouts, Girl Scouts, and Camp Fire Girls. Concerts such as Live Aid and Farm Aid were organized and conducted by volunteers working together for a common cause. Your single effort, small as you think it might be, in concert with others can do wonderful things.

Do you think you want to be a volunteer? Before you answer that question, let's first look at exactly what makes a volunteer. Ben Solomon gave an excellent description of a volunteer as someone who helps to the best of his or her abilities some other person, group, or organization without any thought of financial reward. A volunteer is a person who chooses freely to give service to others without pay. Anyone can be a volunteer. Doctors, engineers, secretaries, maintenance workers, teenagers, grandmothers, and school teachers can all be volunteers. They are identified by the way they help others rather than by their educational level, religion, job status or place of residence. As a volunteer you become a unique "staff member" of the agency or cause you have agreed to help.

If you decide to become a volunteer, you will join the ranks of the millions of Americans that volunteer their time each year to a wide range of organizations and causes. Kathy Wolf [1988] reported that 8.4 billion hours of work are volunteered in the U.S.

each year. That represents a dollar value of $645 billion. No matter how many professional staff members are hired, organizations such as 4-H, Girl and Boy Scouts, public recreation agencies, hospitals, nursing homes, the Red Cross, and other social service agencies will always need volunteers. In many instances, these agencies can't deliver their services without volunteers. Volunteers and professional staff constitute a team working to provide a better quality of life for all involved.

# Rewards and Benefits of Volunteering

Although there are cases where volunteering has done more harm than good to both an agency and the volunteer, volunteering is generally considered beneficial to both parties. Many executives would not eliminate volunteer positions from their work force even if they were given the budget to hire an all professional staff. They recognize that volunteers bring to the job skills and attitudes, a personal dedication, and a dynamic force that could not be bought at any price. As a volunteer, you can expand, extend, and improve the program. You can give the agency a deeper and wider reach into the community that supports it. Volunteers keep the agency sensitive to community and client needs. You can help the community become more responsible for the progress and success of the agency. Because volunteers come from local neighborhoods, they can promote contacts with important citizens for the benefit of the agency. You present an excellent example of service to others, simply because you are a volunteer. Good volunteers help recruit other volunteers into the program. The rewards and benefits of volunteering go well beyond what you can do for an agency. You will receive many personal benefits and rewards if you volunteer.

As a volunteer, you may find ways to meet certain personal needs that are not being met in other aspects of your life. Many people are able to meet recognition and group affiliation needs through work as a volunteer. Volunteering can provide opportunities for you to broaden your social life and help you meet interesting people. You could also have a chance to become visible and influential in your community. Successful volunteer efforts are often reported in local newspapers, and many organizations recognize volunteers who have done an outstanding job at annual banquets.

Volunteering also makes you feel good. In many volunteer positions, you will have the opportunity to help others that are less fortunate than yourself. A smile on a child's face or a thank you from an elderly couple may be the best reward you receive from volunteering. You can also gain satisfaction from working for a project or cause that you feel is important, such as Students Against Drunk Driving, (SADD) cleaning up the environment, or helping the homeless. There are many causes that originated and continue to grow through volunteer efforts. Programs like SADD were started by people who recognized that a problem existed in their community and they wanted to do something to solve it. Being committed to a cause can be very rewarding as you see the results of your efforts.

Another benefit of volunteering is that it can provide a way for you to explore a new career or widen your professional contacts. For example, if you thought you were interested in working in a hospital after high school, what better way to find out the type of jobs that are available, and whether you would like to work in that setting, than to volunteer in a hospital? As a volunteer you can improve your skills, gain insight into the work setting, and expand your knowledge and interests. You can obtain experiences that will help you make important career decisions in the future.

Opportunity for leadership training is also available. As a volunteer you cannot command others to follow or cooperate. You must learn how to influence people and motivate them through suggestions and negotiation. Working with the public will provide many opportunities for a volunteer to practice communication skills, motivation, and other leadership skills. Many businesses appreciate the value of volunteer service and encourage their executives to volunteer for community services. The training received as volunteers will help them as they move up the administrative ladder.

Volunteering has many personal and therapeutic values in relation to physical, mental, social, and emotional health. It can undercut boredom, monotony, and loneliness. For many, volunteering is considered a leisure activity.

A school principal who lost her husband devoted herself to making her school a community center, benefitting the entire neighborhood. A businessman, very active in Boy Scouts when asked why he gave so much time, effort, and money to this agency, said "I've got to have something to take my mind off the shirt business." A retired banker volunteered in a hospital and was given the job of cleaning and sharpening instruments. He enjoyed the work immensely and invented new ways of doing the job, saving time and money. He soon had his own laboratory and two assistants. He admitted he was having the time of his life doing something he had created and helping others. It gave him new purpose, new interest, new friends, and renewed health.

As a volunteer, it will be important to select a position that will allow opportunity to provide benefits to the agency and its clients. It is also important to realize that the rewards or benefits you need to receive may change over time. When you feel you are no longer receiving benefits from your volunteer position, then it may be time to change positions. You may need a new challenge.

In summary, volunteering can provide many personal benefits such as:

1.  It can bring you peace of mind, self-respect and the respect of the community. It can bring you prestige and standing among your peers.
2.  It can create self-confidence and personal pleasure for a job well done.
3.  It can fulfill your inner need to belong to something worthwhile, to be wanted, to be needed, to be a part of something highly regarded by society.
4.  You have the opportunity to learn new skills or improve the ones you already have. You can expand your knowledge of many things and develop new interests. Volunteering can stimulate your intellectual activity and general education.
5.  Volunteering can broaden your social life and help you meet interesting people.
6.  It also helps to develop judgment and your leadership potential.
7.  Volunteering has many recreational values. It rapidly

dissipates boredom, monotony, and loneliness while
it helps to develop a sense of individual security.

8.  If you are a professional person, you can broaden
    your business contacts through volunteering.

Are you thinking of volunteering your time to an
organization? You should translate that desire into action,
because you will never be sorry. You are very much needed. The
tradition of volunteerism goes back to the first settlers. They
were always ready to work together to meet the challenges of the
new world. You too can use your talents and skills to help others.
No one can receive "higher pay" than those who work for others,
who concern themselves with others' problems, and who sacrifice
their own time and effort to make the world a little better place
in which to live.

# The Basic Essentials of a Volunteer

Although volunteering is very rewarding, it is not an
experience you should enter into unless you have the basic
essentials to be a volunteer. First, you should honestly want to
help others. Volunteers can receive many rewards and
recognitions for their work, but that should be a secondary
motive. You should also be a person of good character who has
high ethical and moral standards. This is essential if you are
working with children. It is important that you will be able to
reflect the ideals and values represented by the agency. You will
not be an effective volunteer if you do not believe in the mission
and goals of the organization. Third, you should have good
work habits that are reflected in characteristics such as being
responsible, dependable, reliable, sincere, honest, loyal, and
conscientious. You are an ambassador for the organization and
your work will reflect on the agency. Often you will be the first
person the program participants will come in contact with. As a
representative of the agency, you should approach your volunteer
position as you would a paid position. Fourth, you should be
emotionally stable, with an even temperament and an ability to
keep your personal problems and worries separate from your
job. If you have personal problems that may have a harmful
effect on those you lead, then volunteering is not for you. Finally,

you should realize your own limitations and be willing to attend training. As a volunteer, expect to be supervised and given directions by a paid staff member or another volunteer.

There is a price to pay for volunteering. Are you willing to pay it? Volunteering requires sacrificing time and is often rather inconvenient. You'll have to take on responsibilities and obligations to and for other people. It is generally a serious business, especially if you have to work with people you may not like. Disappointments arise, disillusionment, frustration, and criticism will be part of the price. There will be times when you will wonder whether you are doing any good or just wasting your time. There will be times when you won't see any immediate results of your hard work. Be patient. It may be a long time before the results of your good work are evident. Ms. Logan is an example of someone who saw the results of her hard work.

The night was rainy and Ms. Logan was tired and discouraged. As she prepared to close the center, she heard a knock on the door. Opening the door she saw Mary standing there. "Ms. Logan, I have to see you right away. My church is sending me to camp for two weeks, so I don't need the money I saved to go to camp. I want to give my $10.00 to some other little girl who can't afford to go to camp." Ms. Logan's heart sang, her frustrations and fatigue were forgotten. What she had tried to implant in the minds of the Girl Scout members had borne fruit. A volunteer does more than her job! Ms. Logan was a leader!

# Beware of Myths about Volunteers

Although many agencies have benefitted from using volunteers, there are still many myths about volunteers. Niepoth [1983] outlines several myths about volunteers that are counterproductive to the effective and full utilization of volunteers. If possible, avoid volunteering for agencies that have staff who still believe the myths discussed below. Their views are out-of-date and could impact on the type of volunteer experience you have.

Perhaps one of the most widespread myths about volunteers is that they are a source of free labor because they do not receive a paycheck. However as the saying goes, there are no free lunches in this world. Volunteers are not free. An agency must be committed to allocating staff time and other resources to the supervision, training, and general support of volunteers. If an agency is not willing to commit resources to its volunteer program, you do not want to volunteer your time to that agency. You need support to be effective.

A second myth is that volunteers do not need training. Nothing is further from the truth. Even volunteers with specific skills need orientation training and updates. Staff often assume that just because someone is educated or has worked for the organization in another capacity, they do not need to be trained. Don't feel you are being insulted if someone requests you receive training before you begin your volunteer assignment. Each volunteer position is unique and there are always new skills you can learn. The absence of training opportunities should be a warning that the staff may not feel that the volunteer positions are important. Investigate the volunteer position further and determine why training is not offered. You may not want to take a position where training is not available, because without proper training you can become frustrated and never reach your potential.

The third myth is volunteers can carry out any function that is done by permanent staff. Many agencies have made the mistake of assuming that volunteers can fill professional staff positions. Although you often have skills and competencies not held by staff, as a rule you should not be asked to replace a paid staff member. This is not to say that you are not capable or valuable to the agency. You bring to the agency many benefits that could not be duplicated by staff, but you have a unique role in the organization. Beware of volunteer positions that have been created as a way to replace paid staff members.

Another myth is that volunteers cannot be evaluated or dismissed from an assignment. Many feel that if a person gives his or her time freely, their work cannot be evaluated nor can unacceptable behavior be corrected. If you are to provide effective services for an agency, there must be a system of volunteer supervision and evaluation. A volunteer that is not doing his or her job is a detriment. A good volunteer system will contain ways in which staff can provide you with constructive feedback on your performance. Evaluation is important for your satisfaction and development. Everyone should know the areas in which they excel and the areas in which they can improve. A pat on the back and constructive feedback never hurt anyone. The evaluation procedures should also include volunteer dismissal and grievance procedures. The agency should have written procedures that would allow them to dismiss you if you are not doing your job, as well as procedures that you could use if agency staff were not providing support for your volunteer position.

A final myth is that the volunteer program is an isolated unit within an agency. You cannot be effective as a volunteer if you are not considered an important part of the agency. There should be a feeling among the staff that volunteers are resources that they can use to enhance their programs. Professional staff must appreciate your hard work and strive to make you a part of the total operation. You should be eager to be part of the team rather than "just a volunteer."

Becoming a volunteer takes time and effort. Selection of the appropriate position is critical to your success. You want to be involved with an organization that believes in volunteers and the work that they do. You want to work with staff members who believe in getting the maximum use from their volunteers. Staff members with positive attitudes toward volunteers ignore the old myths about volunteers and believe:

1. Volunteers can be a key link to program participants. Volunteers may be able to reach participants paid staff members cannot reach.
2. Services can be extended by using volunteers. Volunteers can assume jobs that staff are currently performing, thus freeing staff members to work on new programs.
3. Volunteers are great people to work with.
4. Participants can be served better by more volunteers.
5. Volunteers should grow and develop new skills as they work with our program. Through training, volunteers can be given more responsibility and complex jobs to do.

Staff members who are not committed to a volunteer program have had bad experiences with volunteers and generally believe:

1. Volunteers are just not dependable.
2. Recruiting, training, and supervising volunteers takes too much time.
3. Volunteers lack commitment to the program.
4. There are few jobs that can be turned over to volunteers. They just do not have the skills to perform a professional's job.
5. Volunteers may be more accepted by participants than staff members. We don't want to lose our jobs because of volunteers.
6. A volunteer program takes valuable resources away from other programs that are more beneficial to the agency.

For a rewarding and successful volunteer experience, make sure the organization you want to work for values volunteers as important resources. You may find yourself headed for failure if you volunteer for an agency that is not committed to its volunteer program.

Good leadership skills, dedication, and determination are the keys to a rewarding experience. Once you have found the right volunteer position, you will be rewarded. As a volunteer you have a great deal to give to people, to the organization, and to the community. You will gradually see your efforts help make your community a better place to live.

If you are serious about being a volunteer, get ready to put your plan into action. You will be joining a fraternity of thousands who give countless hours to help others. Your efforts will be well rewarded with smiles, the learning of new skills, public recognition, and the knowledge that you have improved the quality of life for those you have helped. Chapter Seven will provide insight into how you can put your plan into action and become a volunteer.

# 7

# How to Become
# a Volunteer

Once you have decided that you want to be a volunteer, you need to take steps to make your desire a reality. First decide what type of organization you would like to work for. You may not have a definite idea of the type of volunteer work you would like to do, beyond the fact that you want to be involved in something worthwhile. You can begin by talking to friends and family about the volunteer opportunities they are familiar with. They may be able to suggest agencies you might like to investigate. Reading the local newspaper may also provide some interesting leads. Many papers print a weekly volunteer section in which nonprofit agencies describe their volunteer needs. The volunteer opportunities in a community are limitless. All it takes is a little detective work to find a volunteer position that will meet your needs. There are many social service agencies, nonprofit agencies, and youth agencies that are always in need of volunteers. Volunteer opportunities can be found in all sectors of the community including schools, health agencies, cultural events, prisons, animal shelters, zoos, recreation agencies, public safety, youth agencies such as the 4-H, Boy Scouts, Girls Clubs, the Council on Aging, the Red Cross, and religious organizations. Many communities have a Volunteers' Bureau or Community Council that are aware of the volunteer opportunities in your area. The Volunteer Bureau is generally community-wide and is established to service all public and private agencies desiring volunteers. Its main function is to secure applications from a large number of volunteers and to interview them for possible placement in the local agencies. The bureau can use mass appeals to secure large numbers of would-be volunteers. Special training courses for volunteers also might be conducted by the bureau. Some organizations either do not have access to a volunteer bureau or prefer to recruit their own volunteers so don't limit your search for a volunteer position to the Volunteer Bureau. Contact agencies directly about their volunteer positions. You may be a member of an organization in which you could be interested in volunteering your time. Call the local office or chapter in your area to obtain information about their volunteer needs.

Maybe you have an idea or a project on which you would like to work and it is not being promoted in your community. Perhaps a particular organization can help you get started with that project. Discuss your idea with a friend or a professional who could suggest an organization that might be interested in sponsoring your project.

# Finding a Volunteer Position

Once you have found several agencies that interest you as possible volunteer opportunities, you have to decide what type of volunteer work you would like to do. You can select from hundreds of volunteer jobs that have been identified. They range from administrative positions to unskilled manual labor. Generally volunteer jobs can be divided into the following categories: administrative, face-to-face leader and clerical/operational.

The administrative volunteer can be involved in such activities as fund raising, public relations, policy making, or agency advising. Volunteers could be involved in organizing fund-raising events, writing news releases, speaking on behalf of the agency, serving on a board or commission, or being an advocate. Administrative volunteers can also be master volunteers or middle managers. A master volunteer/middle manager is trained by the agency to assume a training, teaching, or supervisory role with other volunteers or participants. Planning and implementing a program is another role a master volunteer could assume. The clerical or operational volunteer also provides a valuable service to an agency. The jobs performed by a volunteer in this role include various clerical tasks, maintenance, and manual labor. The face-to-face leader or direct service provider is perhaps the most well known volunteer role. These volunteers work directly with program clientele. Little league coaches, Candy Stripers, 4-H Leaders, Girl Scout Leaders, and Meals on Wheels drivers are all considered face-to-face leaders. Through these volunteers, agencies are able to extend their services to a large number of people. Many of the nonprofit agencies could not provide their programs without the dedication of the face-to-face leader volunteer. You can begin your volunteer work in any category depending on your level of experience, interest, and skills. If this is your first volunteer experience you may want to begin with a job in either the face-to-face or clerical categories, and then move up to an administrative position.

Once you decide on the volunteer role you would like, you still have several decisions to make, such as the age group you would like to work with. Do you want to work with young children, teenagers, single adults, or senior citizens, or would you like to have limited contact with the public? If you want to work with children, do you prefer working with middle class children, or might you want to work with the underprivileged? On the other hand, you may want to work with disabled children or maybe with the homebound or hospitalized. Children that have been classified as high-risk can provide a challenge for the right volunteer. The same types of questions can be asked for the adult age groups. Only you know whether you have the skills and desire to work with a special group of people such as the underprivileged, disabled, or high-risk. One area of volunteer work that has expanded over the last ten years is the opportunity to work with adults over 65. Although many older adults are in hospitals, nursing homes, and other institutional settings that depend heavily on volunteers, many healthy senior citizens are joining senior citizen clubs and moving into planned housing developments. Volunteer work with senior citizens will continue to expand in the 1990s.

Before you contact an agency, you must also decide whether you will be applying for a volunteer assignment that is short in duration, or whether you want to commit to a long-term volunteer assignment. If you have never volunteered before or have little time to spend as a volunteer, you may want to look for a volunteer job that has a limited time commitment, such as helping mail the fall program catalog or hosting the next issues forum at the YWCA. If you want a long-term assignment, volunteer to be a scout leader, 4-H club leader, board member, or part-time receptionist.

# The Interview

After you have some idea of the type of volunteer position you might like and have a list of possible agencies, you are ready to take action. The third step involves contacting an agency and applying for a volunteer position. Do not be surprised if you are asked to fill out a volunteer application and come in for an interview. Agencies realize the importance of quality volunteers to their program and have procedures to ensure they only involve the best volunteers in their program. Contact the agency and ask for an appointment with the person who coordinates the volunteer program. This may be an executive, a staff person, or the organization's volunteer coordinator. The interview may take place in an office, or the volunteer recruiter may ask to meet in your home, or at a local meeting place. Meeting away from the office may provide a more relaxed atmosphere and allow the interviewer to see how you act in your own environment. You may not be interviewed alone. Some recruiters prefer to interview a prospective volunteer with a friend present or with a large group of other potential volunteers. Whatever the interview situation, it is important that you prepare for the interview. You need to know something about the agency you have applied to, and you need to have an idea of what you would like to do as a volunteer. Be prompt for the appointment and dress as though you were applying for a paid position. Remember that you are trying to sell your skills and experiences to the agency. Present a realistic picture of your prior experiences and skills, and be prepared to furnish references.

Be honest about your desires, your background, experience, and especially about your reasons for volunteering. Don't hide your limitations concerning home or job obligations. Expose your dislikes, problems, or disabilities that might affect your job performance. Be as objective as you can about your skills and abilities, your interests and hobbies. During the interview, discuss your volunteer job preferences. It is important that you present a clear picture of your needs and expectations. Before you leave the interview, make sure all your questions have been answered to your satisfaction. You need to understand the job requirements and responsibilities as well as the agency's attitude toward volunteers. Remember you want a job that you fit, and that fits you. You want satisfying work that will allow you to grow and learn while you volunteer.

# Volunteer Job Description and Contract

If you are offered a volunteer position, be sure you have a clear idea of the job duties, responsibilities, and purpose. Job responsibilities should be outlined in a job description similar to the one in Figure 7.1. Some people think that a job description is not necessary for a volunteer position because it does not allow the volunteer job to be fit to the potential volunteer. However, a general job description can give you some idea of what the agency is expecting of you if you accept that position. The job description can always be modified later to reflect your talents and interests. If a job description has not been written, write your own after you have been at work for several weeks. A job description should include the following components:

1. Job Title
2. Program Description
3. Direct Supervisor
4. Location
5. Responsibilities
6. Qualifications or Skills Needed
7. Commitment
8. Evaluation

Discuss the job description with your supervisor and if possible have it placed in your file for future reference. Besides your responsibilities, you should also learn how you will be supervised, how you will be trained, what equipment or supplies are needed, and how you can request help if it is needed. This

# TEEN CLUB VOLUNTEER JOB DESCRIPTION

### Program Description

Coordinate the efforts of the youth members of the community center teen club. Assist the youth to plan, conduct and evaluate their meeting and group projects.

### Supervisor

Dennis Vick, Director of Youth Programs, Williamsburg Department of Parks and Recreation, 808 Main Street, Williamsburg, North Carolina 27604. (000) 555-4561.

### Location

Meetings are held in the Winston Community Center, 204 Windel Road., Williamsburg, North Carolina.

### Specific Responsibilities

1. Guide club officers. Orient members on officers' duties. Assist with agenda preparation and general meeting.
2. Recruit parents and other adults to assist the club members in their planned activities.
3. Organize and meet with a club planning committee.
4. Assist club members to develop a yearly calendar of events.
5. Provide opportunities for youth to plan and implement educational programs.
6. Provide opportunities for members to learn and practice leadership skills.

### Qualifications/Skills Needed

1. Have experience working with youth 14 to 18 years old.
2. Have planning and organizational skills.
3. Recruitment skills.
4. Can teach and prepare educational programs.
5. Minimum age 21.
6. Available to attend monthly club meetings.

### Commitment

One year, negotiate each year thereafter. Fifteen (15) hours per month.

### Evaluation

Complete a volunteer self-assessment evaluation form upon completion of the first four months of the assignment. Participate in a program review of the teen club. Participate in the volunteer development review process conducted yearly.

Figure 7.1

information will help you determine if the position is right for you. If you feel you are not qualified for the responsibilities outlined, don't hesitate to turn down the position. There will be other opportunities. Everyone will lose if you promise more than you can deliver or undertake too great a responsibility.

If you accept a volunteer position, you may want to sign a volunteer contract. Many agencies have made the volunteer contract part of the volunteer program. Like the job description, the contract reinforces the responsibilities and obligations you and the agency have agreed upon. If problems arise, the contract can serve as a basis for evaluation. A sample contract can be found in Figure 7.2. The contract also can contain information concerning space allocation, training opportunities, insurance coverage, reimbursement for such things as meals and travel, and recognition.

# Training Opportunities

Once you have accepted a position, you must become familiar with the agency, its policies, procedures, and facilities. Take advantage of the orientation training and in-service opportunities offered by the agency. Take notes, ask questions and discuss problems with other volunteers and professional staff members. A tour of the facilities with another volunteer or professional staff member will also help orient you to your new surroundings.

On the job, be alert, keep eyes, ears, and mind open. Learn to listen and observe others. If you are working with a specific age group or special population, you should spend time reading material that will help you understand the group's unique characteristics and needs. You may find it very helpful to keep a small question book with you at work. When a question arises, write it down and then seek answers to your questions at an appropriate time.

Orientation training is a very important training period because it prepares you for your job with the agency. Training can consist of a single session or a series of sessions. The length of training will be determined by the technical nature of the position. For example, if you wanted to be a volunteer in the hospital flower shop, you would probably not receive more than a few hours of training. On the other hand, if you want to

## VOLUNTEER CONTRACT

_____
Date

Section I.

I, _____, agree to serve as a
_____ from ____ / ____ / ____ to ____ / ____ /
____. I understand and accept the responsibilities of this position. I have read and understand the mission and policies of the Williamsburg Recreation and Park Department. I agree to abide by the policies established by the Williamsburg Recreation and Parks Department. If at any time I cannot fulfill my obligations, I will contact the appropriate supervisor within 24 hours. Failure to carry out my responsibilities or the policies of the department will result in my dismissal from the above position.

Section II.

In-service training will be conducted on ____ / ____ / ____ from _____ until _____ at Biltmore Center. If I cannot attend the training session, I will contact the Volunteer Coordinator and schedule an alternative training date.

_____
Volunteer's Signature

_____
Volunteer Coordinator's Signature

Figure 7.2

volunteer to work at a zoo as a volunteer teacher for the children's program, you might have to complete twenty hours of training before you would be allowed to work as a volunteer. Formal classroom instruction, group workshops, printed material, observations, one-on-one contact, and on-the-job experience can provide the necessary training opportunities. Your orientation training should be designed to accomplish the following objectives [McKinney, 1983, p. V-5]:

- To understand the nature, purpose, and scope of the organization
- To develop a feeling of belonging
- To develop an understanding of the duties included in the job
- To acquire necessary skills, knowledge, and attitudes to perform specific duties
- To understand and appreciate role relationships with co-workers in contest of unit or group goals
- To understand competencies required for job performance and unit or group goal achievement

Orientation training is the first step in your volunteer development. This training, as well as later training, should be tailored to meet your needs and to promote personal growth.

Continuing education or in-service training opportunities should also be part of your volunteer program. Your education should not stop with your orientation training. If your volunteer experience is going to support personal growth, opportunities for skill improvement and leadership development must be made available. Continuing education can be conducted in-house by the agency in the form of seminars, workshops, and printed material. Or, you can attend meetings, seminars and workshops sponsored by outside firms. Some agencies feel that volunteer development is such a critical component in their volunteer system that they require all volunteers to receive a minimum number of training hours per year. Agencies will often pay either all or part of any cost associated with the training sessions. If your agency does not financially support volunteer training, consider attending the training on your own. The knowledge you gain will benefit you in the future. Also do not hesitate to make your supervisor aware of training opportunities that you think might be beneficial. Ask if they will provide financial support. They may decide not to give you the support you requested, but you will never know unless you ask.

As you receive training, remember to keep a record of the type of training you have received, the number of hours received, and any certifications completed. Your agency should keep accurate records on each volunteer, but often information is not recorded. Training information as well as general information about your volunteer work can be useful on your resume.

Another aspect leading to volunteer development is an opportunity to meet with other volunteers and staff. If the agency does not conduct a regular meeting with volunteers, request that one be established. As a group, volunteers can provide support for new volunteers, and feedback to the agency on their volunteer program. A regular meeting between staff and volunteers can also prove to be beneficial. Many large agencies have volunteer associations organized at the state, regional, or national level which their volunteers are encouraged to join. If you have an opportunity to join such an organization, do so. These organizations provide many leadership opportunities and training sessions beyond those provided at the agency level.

# Leadership

As stated earlier, volunteering can provide opportunities for you to improve your leadership skills. Ideally, a volunteer work situation should allow you to advance to higher levels of responsibilities, skill, learning, and influence. For example, you may begin your volunteer experience with the local recreation department as a scorekeeper for Special Olympics. Over the years you could advance from scorekeeper, to chairman of the scorekeepers, to chairman of the Special Olympics, and then to a board member of the recreation department. In each position you gained more responsibility, learned new skills, and gained influence.

As a volunteer, be prepared to put your leadership skills to work. Remember to lead democratically by planning *with* your group rather than *for* them. Be a person who empowers others by using suggestions and influence rather than trying to control by using orders. Get to know your group members as individuals. Learn their names and their interests as soon as possible. As a leader, you must always be prepared. Before an event, check to see that arrangements have been made and assignments have been carried out. Be sure to see that all activities planned by your group conform to the purpose, standards, and procedures of your organization. If for some reason you cannot carry out an assignment, contact your supervisor immediately so a substitute can be found. Others are depending on you, so approach your volunteer position just as you would a full-time position. Just because you are not on the payroll does not mean that you do not perform an important function for the organization. Failure to fulfill your obligation hurts everyone: you, the organization, and the participants.

## Working for Success

If you are a dedicated and hard working person, and your agency has developed a good volunteer program, you should find volunteering a rewarding experience. However don't get discouraged if your job is not what you expected. Sometimes adjustments need to be made in an assignment. If you have a problem with your job, talk it over with your supervisor. Whatever you do, don't hide or ignore the problem. Little irritants have a habit of turning into big problems. Periodically evaluate your progress by asking yourself this important question, "Am I getting from volunteering what I hoped for in the beginning?" If the answer is no, try to discover why not, and then make the necessary changes to ensure you have a rewarding experience. Again, talk to your supervisor or other staff members who can help you in finding a solution to your problem. Have an open mind about your situation and find a solution that is acceptable to both you and the agency. Be willing to accept a new assignment within the agency or resign from your volunteer role if necessary. It is better to recognize that the job you accepted is not what you wanted than to continue in a position you do not enjoy.

Although there are many problems that can occur in your volunteer situation that are beyond your control, there are many unpleasant situations that you can avoid. As a new volunteer, following the advice below will help ensure that you and the agency have a happy and pleasurable experience.

1. Work within your position. Don't try to take over any rights and privileges of the staff leaders, professionals, or other volunteers.
2. Avoid highly controversial subjects and situations that might embarrass your organization, especially projects and subjects related to religion, racial discussions, crime, and partisan politics. Whereas discussion of these topics is sometimes desirable, these subjects must be carefully guided.
3. Obtain permission from your supervisor before dealing directly with other community agencies.
4. If you think someone has a problem, refer then to the correct agency for help. Don't try to be an amateur psychiatrist, psychologist, or physician with members of your group. Diagnosis and treatment of physical, mental, and emotional problems are for specialists. You may do more harm than good.
5. Counsel with parents, police, or teachers regarding an individual group member only within your authority.
6. Don't undertake or promise to perform beyond your ability to produce.
7. If a problem develops with a group or staff member, take your gripes and problems to the supervisor or to the staff meeting. Don't join or form a pressure group against any individual member or any staff worker, or against the agency.
8. Lead with your head, not with your emotions. Decisions made while angry are often regretted.
9. Leave your job or personal frustrations and problems at home. You cannot be an effective leader if you are preoccupied with other problems.
10. Don't gossip or spread rumors about other leaders, professionals, or volunteers.
11. Remember the aims and purposes of your agency and its work. Be sure to keep your group's program in line with them.

If you want to be a volunteer, you will have to take the time to find a volunteer position that you will enjoy. Occasionally, someone may contact you about volunteering for a particular agency or cause, but that does not often happen. Be aggressive – you can't wait to be discovered. If you do, you may spend your whole life wanting to volunteer and never actually doing it. As you search for a volunteer position, use the following rating scale to help determine which position is right for you.

Does Not Exist   Very Complete
1                              5

1. Does the agency have a job description which outlines the qualifications and skills necessary for the position?

1                              5

2. Does the agency provide an orientation program for volunteers?

1                              5

3. Does the agency sponsor an in-service training program for volunteers?

1                              5

4. Does the volunteer position provide the opportunity for meaningful service to the public?

1                              5

5. Does the agency have a volunteer application that must be filled out?

1                              5

6. Does the agency require an interview with all volunteers before they are offered a position?

1                              5

7. Does the agency provide a time when volunteers can meet together to discuss problems, concerns, and ideas?

1                              5

8. Is there a volunteer contract that must be signed before I can begin my job?

1                              5

9. Are the volunteer evaluation and grievance procedures well outlined?

1                              5

10. Are volunteer records kept by the agency?

1                              5

11. Does the agency have a volunteer recognition program?

|       |       |
|-------|-------|
| 1     | 5     |

12. Does the agency provide ways I can advance into other volunteer positions?

|       |       |
|-------|-------|
| 1     | 5     |

13. Will the agency provide financial support for volunteer training held outside the agency?

|       |       |
|-------|-------|
| 1     | 5     |

14. Does this volunteer position meet my personal needs?

|       |       |
|-------|-------|
| 1     | 5     |

15. Does the agency provide a time when volunteers and professional staff can meet to discuss problems or concerns?

|       |       |
|-------|-------|
| 1     | 5     |

16. As a volunteer, will I be covered by the agency's liability insurance?

|       |       |
|-------|-------|
| 1     | 5     |

17. As a volunteer, will the agency reimburse me for expenses incurred while working as a volunteer?

|       |       |
|-------|-------|
| 1     | 5     |

Good luck in your search for the right volunteer position. If the agency does not have a strong volunteer system, be cautious about becoming involved with that program. You know what it takes to be a successful volunteer. All you need to do now is to put your plan into action.

## TEN RULES FOR VOLUNTEERS
## AND PROFESSIONAL STAFF*

| For Professionals | For Volunteers |
|---|---|
| 1. Describe the job as it is. Don't minimize the time or ability it takes. | 1. Understand the job you are undertaking. |
| 2. Offer a well-planned program of training and supervision. | 2. Accept training. Appreciate and contribute your knowledge and experience. |
| 3. Concern yourself with the volunteer as a person, not an object. | 3. Match your interest to the needs about you and therefore to the job. |
| 4. Expect basic ability and reliability, and then build on them sharing understanding. Do not confuse with jargon. Language should enlighten, not confuse. | 4. Serve with faithfulness and continuity, listen for and report new insights about your work. |
| 5. Be ready to place when you recruit. | 5. Discover the position's meaning to the total program of which it is a part. |
| 6. Give the volunteer a significant task. Don't equate volunteers with untrained persons. | 6. Open yourself to opportunities for growth – in skills, sympathy, self-confidence, and responsibility. |
| 7. Inform the volunteer. Make him an insider. | 7. Value your special two-way role as community interpreter. |
| 8. Evaluate with the volunteer. | 8. Contribute to supervision by self-evaluation and a willingness to ask. |
| 9. Trust the volunteer. If your expectations and faith are high, so will be his response. | 9. Give loyalty to your institution, its staff, and its program. |
| 10. Give proper recognition. | 10. Take pride in the volunteer's career. It pays handsomely in treasures of the spirit. |

*McKinney, (1983) Adapted from writings of Dr. Daniel Thursz and Mrs. Leonard Weiner.

# References

Cartwright, D. and A. Zander. 1968. *Group Dynamics: Research and Theory*, 3rd ed. New York: Harper & Row.

Culp, S. 1986. *How to Get Organized When You Don't Have Time.* Ohio: Writer's Digest Books.

Edginton, C. R., and P.M. Ford. 1985. *Leadership in Recreation and Leisure Service Organizations.* New York: John Wiley.

Frazier, A. V. 1986. *Developmental Characteristics of the 4-H Member.* North Carolina Agricultural Extension Service.

Heller, M. P. 1974. *Preparing Educational Leaders: New Challenges and New Perspectives.* Bloomington, IN: The Phi Delta Kappa Educational Foundation.

McKinney, T. T. 1983. *Life Skills For 4-H Leadership Development.* North Carolina 4-H Agents Handbook, North Carolina Agricultural Extension Service.

Niepoth, E. W. 1983. *Leisure Leadership.* New Jersey: Prentice-Hall.

Russell, R. V. 1986. *Leadership in Recreation.* St. Louis: Times Mirrow/Mosby College.

Russell, R. V., 1986. *Instructor's Manual to Accompany Leadership in Recreation.* St. Louis: Times Mirrow/Mosby College.

Schindler-Rainman, E. 1988. *Trends and Changes Affecting the Volunteer World, The Nonprofit Organization Handbook,* second edition. New York: McGraw-Hill.

Swanson, M. T. 1970. *Your Volunteer Program: Organization and Administration of Volunteer Programs.* Iowa: Des Moines Area Community College.

Wolfe, K. 1988. *Volunteerism Newsletter.* Northern Colorado: Sclerosis Society of Colorado, Vol. 5, No. 1.

# Index